THE PENSIONS DISASTER

and how to plan for a secure retirement

Rod Thomas FCA
CEO OF AXIS PROPERTY INVESTMENT

avantis press

First published in England in 2012 by Avantis Press
Gemini Business Centre, 136-140 Old Shoreham Road
Hove, East Sussex, UK BN3 7BD

Printed and bound in the UK by Biddles, part of the MPG Books Group,
Bodmin and King's Lynn

ISBN 978-0-9573403-0-5

Visit www.axispropertyinvestment.com to keep up to date with investment and pension matters and to find out about workshops, seminars and webinars related to this book. You can also register, free of charge and without obligation, for advance notice of new investment opportunities.

Contents

Chapter 1
Introduction

Many of us face hard times, particularly if retirement is approaching. Most of us were brought up to believe that providing for retirement was easy – just hand over a monthly amount to a pension provider; they would invest your money and all would be well. On retirement, you would receive a fairly predictable monthly income that would provide for your needs – at least, at a basic level.

In the last 15 years, this expectation has proved wrong, very wrong. For many reasons that I will explore shortly, most pensions are now woefully inadequate. And yet few people, so far, have chosen to take back control of their pension and find ways to improve its performance.

This is a tragedy and something I feel passionate about. In my view, the entire financial services industry has mislead investors. They have taken large amounts of your money in charges and fees, while offering a very limited number of investment choices that all too frequently have turned out to be poor options.

This approach to investing your money has been the best – and easiest – option for the pensions industry. However, that's not the same as being the best option for you!

I'd like to redress the balance. In this book, I will show you exactly how the present mess has arisen. I will talk about what it means for you and your pension, and I will discuss the many – and better – options for the future.

Taking a different path will enable you to:

1. Take back control of your pension;
2. Improve its performance.

If you have 20 or more years until retirement, choosing an alternative approach will be incredibly effective and easy to do.

Alternatively, you may have a much shorter time to retirement, in which case you will need to move fast and take an aggressive approach to growing your capital. In this case, the changes you make can still have a material impact on your future income – but, where the time is shorter, the greater action you will need to take. The key is not to delay but to act right now; every day that you keep doing the 'same old, same old' will reduce the potential benefit of making changes.

I hope that you find this book stimulating and informative. Most importantly, I hope that you end up with a clear understanding of the options open to you and the benefits that can accrue from changing course and taking control of your future. This book is for you and your benefit.

If you have any questions or comments, I'd appreciate the feedback. Write to me, Rod Thomas, at rod@axiscontact.com

Live with Abundance,

Rod Thomas FCA

Chapter 2

Scary Pension Facts

The Pensions Policy Institute (PPI) does a great job of bringing together critical facts and understandings about the pensions industry and people's – that's yours and mine – provision for retirement. It makes sober reading. Let's start this journey by reviewing the most important data that the PPI and the Scottish Widows' pension survey reveals:

	NOW	IN FUTURE	CHANGE
	12 million	16.4 million (2050)	36% increase
Life expectancy at age 65 (men)	21.1 years	25.8 years (2050)	22% increase
State pension and benefits paid by Government	£84 billion	£189 billion (2035)	125% increase
Basic state pension	£97	£318 (2035)	8% pa
Proportion of working people paying into a non-state pension	Women 37% Men 40%	n/a	n/a
Average amount received by single pensioner from occupation or personal pension	Occupational pension - £121 a week Personal pension - £74 a week	n/a	n/a
Average size of fund used to buy an annuity	£25,874 (2010 data)	n/a	n/a
Average contributions to a private pension as a proportion of average earnings	8.1% (2008 data)	n/a	n/a
Amount of money in funded pensions	£2.1 trillion (2010 data) = 147% of total UK GDP	n/a	n/a
People saving nothing in 2011	20%	n/a	n/a
People not making enough provision for retirement	51%	n/a	n/a
Gross domestic savings	11% of GDP in UK 21% of GDP in Germany	n/a	n/a

What are the key points within this data?

There is a huge amount of money tied up in pensions (£2.1 trillion), most of which has not delivered acceptable performance for 15+ years.

- The average pension 'pot' of £25,874 is unbelievably small – too small to create an acceptable income. At current annuity rates, a man age 65 would receive just £28 income each week, and this would reduce in value every year because of the impact of inflation.

- Most people don't contribute enough to their pension to create a satisfactory income in retirement – unless an average pension income of £74 to £121 a week is enough!

- The state pension is becoming an increasing burden on the state. Moreover, even the current level of £97 per week is simply not adequate to cover even essential needs.

- Increasing life expectancy is adding to the problems of creating an adequate income for life, and this will continue to put pressure on annuity rates.

The bottom line is that the whole provision of pensions is in dire trouble for multiple reasons – and that's before you start considering the dismal performance of your existing pensions in terms of failure in growth, excessive charges and more.

The good news is that there are solutions that can enable you to take control and improve the performance of your pension. My job is to reveal the extent of the problem and then – more importantly – to provide you with alternative options that will enable you to build a much healthier pension pot. You can then create an excellent income which will make your retirement a pleasure and not a trial!

Chapter 3

How do pensions work?

How do pensions work?

Let's start at the very beginning by laying out the basics of how 'traditional' pensions work. My comments here relate to UK nationals living within the UK tax system. Other countries may have different rules.

What is a pension for?

A pension plan is simply a tax-efficient savings plan that is designed to help people provide for their retirement. You save during your working life and receive an income in retirement. Providing for your own financial future after a life of work is a very important concept; it's even more critical today when the Government's ability to provide income for pensioners is being stretched by challenging economic times.

Benefit of tax relief

The single biggest benefit of investing in a pension is the availability of tax relief at your marginal rate of tax:

- If you pay tax at 20 per cent, you contribute only 80p in every £1 that is invested, with the Government making up the difference.
- If you pay tax at 40 per cent, you contribute only 60p in every £1 that is invested.

Also, most of your investments grow in your pension fund free of tax.

These tax benefits can have a huge impact on your investment outcome over a longer period, and this helps to create a far bigger pension that would otherwise be the case.

The 'rules' about how much can be contributed – what tax relief is available and how it is given – change regularly. There is a guide to pension contributions in the Appendix at the back of this book, but please check current rates to ensure that you are working with the most recent information.

Building your pension

Typically, a monthly sum is paid to a pension provider, and this process continues over many years. This amount may be contributed fully by you, or partly by you and your employer. In rare situations, the pension contributions may be contributed entirely by your employer.

These contributions are invested in a limited range of approved investments. For traditional pensions, the investment focus is primarily focused on quoted shares, government gilts and cash. The investment options are defined by the Financial Services Regulations.

Over years, the investment returns are supposed to provide an increasing pension pot that grows until retirement age.

The size of the pot will vary depending on:

- The contributions you make;
- The amount of tax relief;
- The charges you incur;
- The investment returns;
- The time that you invest for.

The general advice is to start saving early in life – and you've made an excellent decision if you have done so already. There is an enormous difference between saving for, say, ten years, 20 years or 40 years because of the power of compound growth.

Just as an example, suppose you were to save £1,000 a year and your investment grew at the rate of five per cent a year: what would your pension pot be worth?

PERIOD OF INVESTMENT	AMOUNT CONTRIBUTED	INVESTMENT GROWTH	TOTAL SIZE OF 'POT'
1 year	£1,000	£50	£1,050
10 years	£10,000	£4,207	£14,207
20 years	£20,000	£15,719	£35,719
40 years	£40,000	£87,840	£127,840

What is illustrated here, very graphically, is that growth massively accelerates after around 20 years of investment. If you are, say, within ten years of the retirement age and have not made adequate pension provision, you still have time to build something worthwhile – but you may need a more aggressive strategy to achieve your goals. I will come to those options later.

Taking your pension

Until fairly recently, there was only one way to take your pension – and this traditional approach is still the most prevalent. You would buy an annuity from a financial services company; this could be the same company that you invested your pension with or a separate investment company.

The annuity is a monthly income for life. The amount you would be offered would be expressed as a percentage of your total pension pot. So, for example, if you were offered an annuity of five per cent on a pension pot of £100,000, you would receive an annual income of £5,000 for life.

The amount of the annuity you would be offered depends on:

- Whether you are male or female;
- The age at which you chose to retire;
- The state of your health (poor health = higher annuity);
- Interest rates and investment expectations from the financial services company;
- The type of annuity (see Page 26)

As you might imagine, the calculations are complex and the market is reasonably competitive, so the annuity can vary considerably between providers.

There are four critical matters to understand about annuities:

1 Once you have made a decision and signed an agreement, there is no going back. This means you can't 'undo' a decision about turning your pension pot into an annuity.

2 There are broad limits around the time you may choose to retire – it is not fixed at 65 – so you need to weigh up whether you want to take your income sooner at a lower level or later at a higher level.

3 The provision of annuities is competitive and there is a likelihood that your own pension provider may not be offering the best deal. Remember, you can shop around.

4 When you 'buy' an annuity, you are effectively giving your capital sum to the annuity provider. This means that you have no 'capital' left, just an income in retirement as defined by the rules you agreed to. If you die before you're 75 years old, you do get a 'money-back' option, which means that your estate will receive the difference between what has been paid out in pension and the capital value of the annuity.

The majority of retiring pension holders still go ahead and purchase an annuity, often receiving poor value from their existing pension company.

Tax-free cash

Within the UK system, retirees can take 25 per cent of their capital sum as a tax-free lump sum on retirement. Clearly, this reduces the size of the pension pot and the income that you can receive in retirement.

Income drawdown

In recent years, however, the Government has realised that annuities are relatively inflexible. This is why it has introduced the concept of 'drawdown'. Drawdown enables investors to avoid taking an annuity; instead, you can take part of your capital (and investment profits) on an annual basis, subject to defined restrictions.

One benefit of drawdown is that, when you die, your remaining capital sum is still an asset of your estate and can be left to your inheritors, less a 55 per cent tax charge.

A second benefit is that drawdown can be more flexible than an annuity, allowing you to cope with fluctuations in your requirements for income – a benefit that is clearly not possible with an annuity. The available income depends on whether you have enough pension income to qualify for 'flexible drawdown' or not (see the Appendix for details).

If you do take a higher income amount than you would receive from an annuity, flexible drawdown may – potentially – increase the risk to you as a pensioner.

In this case, careful professional advice is needed.

Summary

- A pension is a tax-efficient savings plan with rules set out by the Government;

- Up to certain limits, you can contribute to an approved pension and get tax relief at your highest marginal rate (up to 50 per cent);

- Investments inside your pension grow mostly tax free;

- Because of the nature of compound growth, you really see a massive benefit from your savings from around 20 years. So, starting to save early is the ultimate key to building a good pension fund;

- When you retire, you can take up to 25 per cent of the fund value as tax-free cash;

- The balance is used to provide an income through two alternative approaches: annuity or income drawdown.

Chapter 4

Why 'traditional' pensions are a disaster

I'm known for straight talking and so I will put it bluntly: the pension industry has failed on a massive scale to deal with changing conditions, it has lined its own pockets at our expense and it is delivering – generally – appallingly low levels of income in retirement.

For many people – and this may include you – understanding pensions can make the difference between a comfortable life in retirement and a struggle for survival.

For younger people who have many years to go, the pensions' disaster is a massive wake-up call. The level of growth (what growth, I hear!) is simply not going to deliver what you need in many years' time.

In order to understand what can be done about this disaster, we need to start by understanding exactly how it has arisen. So, here are the BIG TEN problems, which I divide into three categories:

Category One - Problems that make it difficult to build an adequate pension 'pot'

- Appalling fund performance;
- Excessive fees and charges.

Category Two - Problems that make it difficult to obtain an adequate income after retirement

- Increased life expectancy;
- Inflation;
- Low Interest rates.

Category Three - Other problems with the current pension system

- Lack of control;
- Limited asset choices and over-conservative investment processes;
- Loss of assets for inheritance purposes;
- Lack of flexibility after retirement.

Category One problems

Fund performance

Your monthly contributions have been invested by your pensions company, and the annual profit is added each year to build your pension pot until you retire.

There are three key factors to remember about how pension companies operate: because they invest huge amounts of money (£2.1 trillion in the UK right now), they naturally have to invest in assets that are themselves substantial. They are also restricted by government legislation and they are naturally conservative investors – losing money for their pension contributors is not a good idea!

So, traditionally, most investment has been in the shares of large public companies, government gilts (loan notes) and cash.

What does this mean in 'real life'? To get a sense of just how bad things are, we need to look at some actual numbers and dates. Here is some data on the FTSE 100 Index – the most comparable index of leading UK company shares – which makes up much of the investment strategy of pension companies.

Today's Index - June 2012	5287
Index at end of 2000	6223
Index at end of 1997	5136

To help you grasp the terrible underlying performance of **your** pension, you simply have to understand that – over the last **15** years – any investment in a basket of FTSE 100 companies has gone absolutely NOWHERE and made NOTHING – zero, nada, nothing. Not one per cent of growth, not just in a year, but in that entire 15 year period.

And, this is before the impact of **charges** and **inflation.**

As a result of this appalling performance, most pension pots have been shrinking, and they continue to get smaller year-on-year – exactly the opposite of what you need!

If you just needed one reason to stop doing what you are doing and invest a different way, the lack of fund performance should be **No 1** on your list.

Exorbitant charges and fees

You probably know that the pensions industry is renowned for the high level of fees and charges it makes. Start-up fees, annual management fees, performance fees, trading costs, exit fees and more – they are all likely to make an appearance in your pension plan.

Last year, BBC Panorama broadcast a program that investigated pension charges; the results were truly shocking. Money Management's latest pension survey echoed the findings of Panorama. Before I reveal the results of these investigations, I want to give an insight into what existing pension contributors imagine is happening with fees.

When I ask people what charges they expect to pay over the lifetime of their pension, most offer an answer in the range of five to ten per cent. In other words, most people guess that as much as ten per cent of their total contributions is consumed in charges.

Taking this estimation, if you contributed £200 a month for 25 years, your total investment would be £60,000. Fees of ten per cent would reduce your contributions to £54,000. Although you might think these fees are high, you could probably live with them – provided that the fund was growing well as a result of good investment performance.

What do you think is a reasonable level for pension charges? Two per cent of your total contributions? Five per cent? Ten per cent – or more?

Let's take a look at what Panorama and Money Management found.

Firstly, Panorama: they asked a number of pension providers – including some of the largest banks –what was the level of charges and fees they levied in total, expressed as a percentage of the pension contributions over the lifetime of the pension. In other words, the same question that I asked investors above.

The worst offender, which I shall not name here, took an astonishing 80 per cent of your total contributions in fees and charges!

I repeat that: 80 per cent of your contributions were not invested; they were taken in various ways as fees and charges. Personally, I consider that criminal.

Money Management looked at the issue a little differently. They examined the impact of fees on the overall performance of the pension fund, and found that some pension companies took such high fees that the fund performance fell by around 25 per cent.

Fees knock 25pc off the value of your pension fund.
Illustration by Howard McWilliam - www.mcbill.plus.com

This fall in fund value includes, not only your contributions, but also the investment profits generated over the years.

As an example, the Money Management Pension Survey looked at a person saving £200 a month for 25 years. With Scandia, this should have resulted in a pension pot of £157,494 (£60,000 of capital contributed and £97,484 of investment profit). Because of charges, however, the pension 'pot' was reduced to just £120,050 – a reduction of 25 per cent. In fact, the charges reduced the investment gain from £97,484 to £60,050, a reduction in profits of 38 per cent!

How do you feel about almost 40 per cent of your investment return being taken in fees and charges?

Here are two outrageous consequences of the way that fees are taken and paid, beyond the sheer scale of them:

Firstly, the annual management fee, charged on the fund value, is always taken – even if your pension pot loses money.

Secondly, your Independent Financial Advisor (IFA) receives a share of the fees each year. Do you really think that they would ever genuinely recommend you switch your pension away from your current provider – especially if it meant that they lose commission for years ahead? As we shall see later, it may cause you sleepless nights when you decide (if you haven't already!) to take control of your pension, while your advisor is recommending that you leave things as they are!

The mishmash of an appalling fund performance and ridiculously high fees and charges combine to result in a very poor pension pot. In most cases, people's traditional pension pot is worth less now than it was five, ten or even 15 years ago.

Example: poor fund performance with excessive charges

Let's finish this section with a realistic example. I will look at two scenarios. In both cases, I will assume a 20-year investment term, with fees that take a modest 15 per cent off the final capital sum. The first scenario will assume five per cent annual growth, compounded. The second – which is close to the actual average result in the UK over the last 20 years – assumes zero growth.

In both cases, we will assume pension contributions of £1,000 a year (cash paid) with tax relief at 20 per cent. This means that the pension company actually receives £1,250 per year:

Scenario One - Five per cent annual growth for 20 years

Value of contributions from you	£20,000
Added from tax relief	£5,000
Total contribution over 20 years	£25,000
Value of investment profit at 5% pa	£19,650
Total pension pot before fees	£44,650
Potential cost of fees	£6,697
Net value of pension	£37,952
Increase in capital over 20 years	89%

Scenario Two - Zero per cent annual growth for 20 years

Value of contributions from you	£20,000
Added from tax relief	£5,000
Value of contributions over 20 years	£25,000
Value of investment profit at 0% pa	Nil
Total pension pot before fees	£25,000
Potential cost of fees	£3,750
Net value of pension	£21,250
Increase in capital over 20 years	6%

The overall picture is a disaster when growth is non-existent over an extended period, as has been the case in the UK roughly since the turn of the 21st century – around 12 years ago!

Category Two problems

As if poor fund performance and exorbitant fees weren't bad enough, let's now turn our attention to the second category of problems. These relate to the issue of gaining an acceptable income from whatever pension pot you have.

Before I turn to this issue, here's a quick reminder that the pension pot you have accumulated during your working life now needs to provide an income for your retirement until you die. Most people will achieve this by buying an 'annuity' – that is, an annual income for life.

More about annuities

As I've already discussed, when you purchase an annuity you effectively sell your pension pot to an annuity provider in return for a guaranteed income. I've already looked at the factors that influence the amount of annuity you will receive, but I want to translate this into real numbers and see what's happened over the last few years.

There are several different kinds of annuity that are available:

Level income, single life

This is the most straightforward. You receive a fixed income paid monthly until you die, after which it stops.

Level income, joint life

You receive a fixed income, but – if your partner survives you – they will receive an income until they also die. However, it is customary for your partner's income to be substantially lower than the income you received.

Rising income, single life

You may request a rising income, which is sometimes linked to inflation or at a pre-agreed level of increase. Again, the income stops when you die.

Rising income, joint life

Similar to 'Rising income, single life', but with the benefit that your surviving partner will receive some income until they also die.

Guaranteed payment

Some annuity providers offer a guaranteed payment period, in which the income is made available even if the recipient of the annuity dies. These guaranteed periods are typically three or five years.

To start with, as you might expect, the annuity provider issues payments at a lower level in order to accommodate various possible factors, such as whether you want to be paid more income in the future, or to increase the potential time for payment, or to provide a guarantee.

What does this mean in 'real life'?

For a realistic example, let's take a 65-year old man in normal health. Annuity rates vary considerably over time and, as you would imagine, there are huge variations between providers. At the time of going to press, the 'best buy' tables show the following return for our 65-year old, based on a pension pot of £100,000:

TYPE OF ANNUITY	AMOUNT
Single life, level	£5,971
Single life, escalation at 3% pa	£4,131
Joint life 50%, 3% escalation	£3,614

I'm not sure about you, but this strikes me as an unbelievably small return for a pension pot of £100,000 – which, in itself, is **FOUR** times the national average pot of £25,784 (Pension Policy Institute data).

Historically, the annuity route seemed like a good idea. For a man age 65 who retired in the mid-1990s – say, around 1995 – the income in retirement was far higher. A £100,000 pension pot at that time would have offered an income of around £15,000 a year.

Today, this is down to just under £6,000 – a massive 60 per cent **FALL** in the income you can expect from retirement. And, if you have just the average pension pot of £25,000, then you will end up with the paltry amount of £28 a week!

So, how has this massive fall in annuity rates happened? Let's first understand the issues, then we can design the 'perfect pension' that will offer better solutions and a more empowering future.

Increasing life expectancy

As I revealed in the table at the beginning of this book, life expectancy is increasing. Here are the numbers again:

LIFE EXPECTANCY	NOW	IN 2050	CHANGE
Male (at age 65)	21.1	25.8	22% increase
Female (at age 65)	23.8	28.2	18.5% increase

Since you buy an annuity for life, this level of increase in life expectancy has a major impact on the ability of the annuity provider to keep paying you. As a result, the annual income they offer has fallen and will continue to fall as life expectancy increases further.

Low interest rates

The annuity provider has to guarantee your income for life. Consequently, they have to pick super-safe investments that, above all else, do not risk your capital. If they get that wrong, then their ability to pay your income will diminish very quickly.

This means that much of their investment will be in government gilts (loans to the Government). These are generally considered the safest investment – at least in our first world country.

The problem is that, with our current record low interest rates, the rate of return on government gilts has also fallen. With the official Bank of England rate at a historic low (0.5 per cent at the time of writing), this has had a massive impact on potential returns that annuity providers can generate.

DATE	AVERAGE RATE OF INTEREST ON 3 MONTH TREASURY BONDS (BANK OF ENGLAND DATA)
1995	6.37%
2011	0.48%

This is a fall in revenue of 92 per cent over the last 17 years. Quite astonishing.

Impact of inflation

As we have seen, the standard annuity is level income and takes no account of inflation. If you do want to provide for inflation, then the starting income is typically some 30 per cent lower than you would receive with a level income.

You are effectively caught between a rock and a hard place: either reduce the income you need now even further, or worry about not having enough later on because of the impact of inflation.

So, what exactly is the impact of inflation?

Let's suppose inflation averages at three per cent a year, and that you start with an income of £100 a week. What would that be worth, in real terms, after 20 years? Any guesses?

Well, you would need the equivalent of £160 a week in 20 years' time to buy the same things that £100 buys today. In other words, since you would not have this increased amount, you would face a shortfall of around 40 per cent in your standard of living.

This is a scary number. When we are working, our incomes often rise – either because of inflationary increases or job advancement – and so the impact of inflation is hidden to some degree. However, retirement on a fixed income can be a killer, particularly now we are all living longer.

Category Three - Other problems with the current pension system

Lack of control

With a traditional pension, you have no control over investment choices or timing. This was a positive when pension companies continued to achieve good growth, in spite of their charges! It is less than good now that performance is dire and most people have pension pots that are falling.

While you might have been happy to leave your pension investment choices to others in the past, taking back control is, frankly, the first and most important step to fixing these problems.

Limited asset choices and the over-conservative investment process

Our Government, in its wisdom, heavily restricted the asset choices that pension companies could make. This was done in an effort to ensure some protection for your money. An admirable idea, but it backfired when the assets that your pensions were invested in – mainly shares – took a tumble that has lasted 15 years!

The situation has been made worse by the involvement of the Financial Services Authority (FSA). The FSA governs the activity of Independent Financial Advisors (IFAs). The FSA does two things that get in the way of good investment decisions and recommendations from your IFA.

The first problem is that the FSA categorises everything into regulated and unregulated investments – and it frowns heavily upon any IFAs that recommend 'unregulated' investments. If an IFA does recommend an unregulated investment, it faces additional questioning and possible censure from the FSA. None of this would matter if all unregulated investments were hugely risky; but did you know that your own personal house is an 'unregulated' investment?

So, in theory, if you asked your IFA whether it's a good idea to buy a house for your own use, many of them might actually say 'no' – purely because they are complying with FSA guidelines! This precludes many IFAs from recommending assets that would make very good sense in your portfolio, but which fall outside the FSA's 'regulated' banner.

The second problem is about portfolio management. The FSA sets 'guidelines' for how a portfolio should be made up. These guidelines advise that commercial property should not form more than 15 per cent of a portfolio. And, as for residential property, student property, alternative investments and much more, there is no recommendation for inclusion into a portfolio at all.

Let's see how this pans out in practice. I have a close friend who is in the wholesale business. Some years ago, he put all his savings on a down payment for a freehold warehouse. This decision meant he avoided paying rent, it fixed his costs and, over the following 20 years, he would pay off the whole bank loan.

When he retires, he will either close or sell the business. He will own a substantial freehold asset, free and clear, with the option to rent it out for a growing income or sell it and reinvest elsewhere. He could even remortgage a small percentage to release some capital and still keep a positive cash-flowing asset.

However, this freehold is his entire pension. It took all his savings to make the deposit. Was it a good decision? I believe so. However, no IFA would ever recommend it because it was 100 per cent of his portfolio and way over the 'recommended' limit of 15 per cent for commercial property.

What a lot of nonsense! The IFAs, who are supposed to provide financial advice, are constrained – firstly by government rules that were made years ago, and secondly by an inflexible and unrealistic Financial Services Authority, which sets 'recommendations' that you override at your peril.

Loss of assets for inheritance purposes

For me, one of the biggest concerns about the present pension system is that, when you buy an annuity, you trade your capital sum for an income. Until recently, this meant that when you died your capital sum was 'lost' and not available to your beneficiaries.

This is bad. Really bad. You've spent many years building a capital sum and now you're losing it all in return for a pretty poor income. Why shouldn't you be able to invest the capital sum and then receive income, while maintaining or even increasing your capital base?

This problem has been recognised within the industry and, recently, a new type of 'capital protected' annuity has become available. This means that, if you die before you reach 75, the annuity provider will return to your estate the difference between the amount paid in pension and the amount of the capital sum you had to buy the annuity.

Let's look at an example. Suppose your pension pot was £100,000 and this bought you an annuity of £5,500 a year at the age of 65.

If you died aged 70, you would have received five years of pension at £5,500 a year.

This is a total of £27,500. Your estate would benefit for a repayment of £100,000 – minus the £27,500 – which is £72,500. Your estate would then be liable for a penalty tax charge of 55 per cent on the amount repaid.

Although these capital protected annuities are a welcome step forward, they still suffer from two major problems:

1) If you choose to take one, you will be offered a lower income in return for the capital protection. Since the income from a regular annuity is very poor, this could tip the balance into not having enough to live on.

2) If you die at the age of 75 or older, the capital protection is finished and you still lose the rest of your capital!

The sensible alternative is to avoid the annuity route altogether and opt for income drawdown. By doing this, your assets stay invested and can continue to grow. Moreover, when you die, your dependants and/or inheritors will continue to benefit from the capital sum remaining – either as a pension paid to dependants, or the return of the remaining capital sum to your estate (less attributable taxation).

Frankly, in my opinion, anyone who opts for an annuity, given its poor value and loss of capital, has taken no responsibility for understanding what is happening to their pension fund.

Lack of flexibility after retirement

If you choose to buy an annuity, you lose all flexibility after retirement. You do have a 'one-off' option of taking up to 25 per cent tax-fee cash from your pension pot. However, once you have committed to the annuity, that's it.

The problem with this situation is that it doesn't enable you to take extra income one year, or even generate another capital release. This could be a real problem if, say, you needed an expensive operation, wanted to take a long holiday, or maybe had some repairs to do on your house.

If you decide to take income drawdown, the parameters are a little more flexible, but they are still very restrictive.

Summary

- Pensions, over the last 15 years, have been a disaster for most people;
- There are 11 major problems, which combine to make it difficult to build an adequate pension fund to start with, and then to create the income you need;
- Lack of control is a big issue;
- Performance of the underlying fund is another major issue;
- And, for many pensioners, losing your pension fund in return for an annuity means that you have nothing left to leave for your dependents.

Chapter 5

Choosing the right strategy for holding your investment

As I'm focusing on pensions and retirement in this book, you may have assumed that I will only talk about holding your investment in a 'wrapper' that qualifies for tax relief, i.e. a pension of one kind or another.

That is not the case. We need to consider TWO possibilities:

1. Holding your assets inside a pension;

2. Holding your assets outside a pension, without the benefit of favourable tax treatment.

At this stage, you may think this is a 'no-brainer' decision, with the balance heavily weighted towards the benefit of the tax relief for pensions. After all, surely the whole idea of providing for your future is to use the tax-efficient system of approved pension wrappers. However, the reality is not so simple and we need to consider the benefits – and drawbacks – of each option.

There is no one, single right approach. Many investors hold assets in a mix of vehicles, both within and outside the pension system.

Why hold assets outside a pension?

No more pension allowance

You have used up your pension allowance according to the rules. This might be because you have hit the total lifetime allowance, or you have fully invested in accordance with your income. It could also be because you are not creating relevant earnings and, therefore, your pension contributions are capped at £3,600 a year (as at 2012).

You have cash savings available

Maybe you have some savings which you don't want to lock up for ever in a pension, but you are willing to make them work harder for you by investing in other assets.

Total flexibility

If you keep your assets outside your pension, you can draw the income you like, raise money against them, sell them at will, and have total flexibility for the future. If you are uncertain about any aspect of your life, this freedom to make choices is extremely important.

Providing for your inheritors

Most assets within a pension will either be lost (as with the purchase of an annuity), potentially lost, or subject to harsh taxation if they are in income drawdown. If you are buying to provide an income during your lifetime, while leaving the asset to your inheritors, then staying outside the pension framework is vital.

Investing in assets that can't be placed in a pension

There are many assets – primarily residential property – that can't be placed in a pension. In this case, keeping the asset outside the pension net is the only choice. If there are good reasons for choosing that asset (and there often are!), the only option open to you is to hold it outside the pension net.

Gaining higher performance

You may be in a position to gain higher returns from an asset that doesn't qualify for pension treatment, but still will show higher returns than assets within a pension. This is a critically important issue and something that many investors are blind to.

Let's take a real-life example. At the time of writing, my company is offering a hotel investment in the USA that offers a guaranteed annual net income of 25 per cent for the next four years. However, this investment does not qualify for inclusion within a pension.

In this case, it is not because of the type of asset, but because the developers have not chosen (and don't need!) to do the work to get the investment approved.

Now, let's say that you qualify for tax relief at 40 per cent, and you invest in an asset that yields eight per cent per annum – an exceptionally high figure by pension standards. Your pension will show a yield of 11.2 per cent per annum because the government is effectively contributing 40 per cent to your pension.

However, even after tax relief, you are not even reaching half the investment return of an alternative asset that is held outside a pension. This is before deducting up to 25 per cent of your growth in fees and charges!

I could show you many similar examples of high-income assets that will generate a far greater return outside a pension than most – if not all – investments within a pension.

You want income now

If you want to earn income today, and you have years before retirement, what's the point of putting the asset into a pension plan? You have precluded yourself from taking the income now!

It's far better to purchase with your cash savings, or borrow on other assets, to purchase – and benefit from – the income stream immediately.

Benefit from leverage

For some asset purchases, particularly those that are property-related, it is usually possible to borrow heavily against the asset. Providing that the income from the asset (such as rent) can cover the repayments and leave you with positive cash flow, this is – in a rising market – an excellent strategy for building capital quickly. Borrowing against property assets can be as high as 75 per cent of the asset value.

You do have the ability to borrow with some pensions – and I will look more closely at these later. However, such borrowing is limited to 50 per cent of the value of the fund. In many cases where the same asset is available both inside a pension wrapper and also for personal purchase, the borrowing facility is limited to cash buyers and not for buyers within a pension.

Let's see how this works. As an example, I will assume that it is 20 years to retirement and (by chance) you chose to invest 20 years earlier. So, at this point, no money has been paid out of your pension; it is all retained within it.

The model is a little simplistic, since we have not taken into account any increases in rent or the impact of reinvesting the income. However, these simplifications do not change the significance of the results.

ASSUMPTIONS	
Property price	£100,000
Property price growth per year	5% pa (UK has averaged 8% over last 50 years)
Net rental	£7,000
Interest on borrowing	4% pa

CRUNCHING THE NUMBERS	OUTSIDE PENSION	INSIDE PENSION
Leverage	75%	Nil
Property value	£100,000	£100,000
Borrowing	£75,000	Nil
Tax relief	Nil	£40,000
Net cost	£25,000	£60,000
Property value after 20 years	£265,330	£265,330
Income for 20 years (no increase)	£140,000	£140,000
Interest payments	£60,000	Nil
Income before tax	£80,000	£140,000
Tax on income at (say) 20%	£16,000	Nil
Net income after tax	£64,000	£140,000

In this example, the property shows a capital profit of £165,000.

In addition, there is a net profit of £64,000 after tax from rental income if it is held outside a pension, or £140,000 if it is held inside a pension.

However, the capital that was originally contributed is different. So, what does all this mean?

RESULTS	OUTSIDE PENSION	INSIDE PENSION
Capital profit on property	£165,330	£165,330
Profit from rental	£64,000	£140,000
Total profit	£229,330	£305,330
Capital contributed	£25,000	£60,000
Return on investment	**917%**	**508%**

The lesson to learn here is that, despite getting 40 per cent tax relief on the initial contributions to the pension, and despite the investor having to pay tax on income generated from rents through the period, the return on investment **outside the pension wrapper** is almost **double** the return of that inside the pension wrapper! This finding will stun many investors who have never analysed the interplay of tax relief and leverage before.

As well as this much higher return on investment, there is also the flexibility of what to do with the asset after retirement. If it is outside the pension wrapper, you can sell it and take the capital. Sure, you would pay capital gains tax (CGT) on the profit at either 18 per cent or 28 per cent (as at 2012), but this is frankly a low taxation rate.

Or, you can keep the property and benefit from the income it generates.

If you have your property inside the pension, you are committed to the income alone, with little prospect of getting the capital released at any stage until death – and, even then, only in a heavily taxed and punitive way.

It's only a few years until retirement

Perhaps the greatest benefit of the pension system and its generous tax relief is the opportunity it offers you to build capital inside a pension wrapper without tax deductions. However, this works best over a long period. If you have only a few years left until you retire, then much of this benefit is never received.

With perhaps five years or so to retirement, it can be counterproductive to tie assets up in a pension wrapper that restricts the freedom of what you can do with them. On the other hand, keeping assets outside a pension is financially more flexible and probably offers a higher investment return.

Why hold assets inside a pension?

By now, you may be surprised by the many benefits of holding assets outside a pension wrapper. It's not all one-way, however, and I want to examine the reasons why you might choose to invest (or maybe 'have to' without choice) inside a pension.

Company schemes

Perhaps your company or organisation provides a pension scheme into which they contribute an amount, as well as you. This can be very beneficial because they are effectively saving part of your salary in a tax-efficient manner. It's possible you have no choice over this – but even if you did, staying inside a company scheme can often be a good idea.

Defined benefit schemes

In the Appendix, I describe what a defined benefit scheme is and what's happened to it. Essentially, it offers a guaranteed final pension, typically offering a percentage of your final salary that has been calculated in various ways.

In today's difficult economic climate, the investment performance of many of these kinds of funds has failed to deliver. As a result, thousands of schemes are now in deficit. What matters to you is that, provided the company that offers the guaranteed pension stays in existence, in most cases you will get paid a pension that bears no relation to the value of the assets that support it. In effect, you may get far more than the underlying investments can validly justify.

If you are in, or have been offered, a defined benefit scheme, treasure it! Your pension benefits will often be far higher than the performance and value of the underlying investment pot will warrant.

Modest savings

Many of the excellent asset choices I will consider later are really only workable if the pension pot reaches a substantial size. The assets often need a lump sum to get started, so if you are making only modest savings every month, it may not be possible to invest in the assets I will look at. In that case, a pension scheme can be the best bet.

High rate taxpayers

The higher the tax rate, the more the Government contributes. So, if you pay tax at the marginal rate of 40 or 50 per cent, then the favourable tax treatment will certainly help to build a useful capital sum. The calculations are less clear for lower rate taxpayers who do not financially benefit so much from government contributions to their pension.

Long time to retirement

As we have seen, if you have a short time to retirement, then the benefits of an investment growing inside a pension are difficult to show. On the other hand, if you have 20 years or more to retirement age, then the benefits of the pension system are clearly more favourable.

Combining the right pension with the right investment choices

Do not assume that all pensions are the same. In previous chapters, I hope I have comprehensively destroyed the notion that the traditional pension scheme investment process is working. It quite clearly isn't. However, there are alternative pension wrappers that offer much more flexibility and greater investment choices. Much of the rest of this book is dedicated to exploring the benefits that will accrue from making the right investment choices inside the best pension wrapper.

You are already in a scheme!

It is very possible that you are already in one or more pension schemes. These can be 'frozen' pensions to which you no longer contribute, or current schemes to which you currently contribute.

If the pension is frozen and you are pre-retirement, then the question is not if you should invest inside or outside the scheme. You are already invested! The big question, and the one we shall discuss shortly, is: what type of scheme should you be invested in and what assets should you hold? Both of these are critical questions that demand serious thought.

If you are in a current scheme, then you need to ask the same questions as above: are you in the right scheme, and are you invested in the most appropriate assets? If you are not (and most people aren't), then now is the time to switch.

You will also need to decide whether to stop, maintain or increase contributions.

Let's be clear here. In the UK right now, there is around £2.1 trillion already invested in pension funds. That's equivalent to 147 per cent of the UK's GDP (gross domestic product – the annual output of the entire economy).

Most of this £2.1 trillion is invested in poorly performing pension schemes, run by companies that are imposing outrageous charges and fees and which have shown little ability to provide the income you need in the future. It's time to take control!

Summary

- You can hold assets for retirement outside as well as inside a pension;
- Many savers don't consider the benefits of keeping full control by owning assets personally;
- Some assets (such as residential buy-to-let property) can only be held outside a pension scheme;
- If you don't have much relevant income, but you do have money to invest, then holding the asset personally may be the only option;
- A good strategy can be to combine assets held inside and outside a pension wrapper.

Chapter 6

Introducing SIPPs - A pension made for the 21st century

By this stage, you may be full of uncertainties, particularly if you hold a 'traditional' pension. I hope you have understood the many ways in which pension schemes are failing. You may also be wondering whether your future investments would be better off **outside** a pension scheme.

Well, it's time to leave the bad news behind and concentrate on the future; it's time for you to take control over your own prospects. Once you begin to get involved in making decisions, your future will be much brighter!

As far back as 1989, the government of the day realised that there were huge limitations and problems with existing pension schemes, and so it began to introduce alternatives. I want to focus on one of these alternatives, SIPP schemes. Although SIPPs have recently celebrated their 21st birthday, it wasn't until the last five years that they began to make an impact on the overall pension market.

Today, SIPPs are the preferred way for astute investors to manage their pension arrangements.

SIPP - Self-invested personal pension

The rationale behind SIPPs was twofold:

- To provide investors with more control and decision-making power;
- To enable a broader selection of investments to be chosen.

With SIPPs, most of the pension rules remain identical in terms of qualifying contributions, but other elements are very different.

The best way to think about SIPP pensions is to think of them as a shopping trolley into which you place your chosen investments. The

SIPP 'container' is separate from the investments that you choose to put inside it.

A SIPP works just the same as any other personal or stakeholder pension in terms of tax benefits, contribution limits and retirement options. You make contributions that are boosted by tax relief, leave the assets to grow (mostly tax free) and then, on retirement, you can take a tax-free lump sum and a taxable income from the capital that remains in the pension pot.

THE FIVE MAJOR BENEFITS OF A SIPP

* Freedom and flexibility - Take control and make your own decisions;
* Cash flow - Contribute when you want, as much or as little as you want (within defined limits) to suit your particular circumstances;
* Choice - Ability to select from a wide range of investment options;
* Value for money - Reduce the huge fees and costs that most 'traditional' pension schemes charge;
* Inheritance - Make it easier to pass your pension to your heirs.

So, what do these benefits achieve?

Improved performance of your pension, resulting in a bigger pension pot and more income in retirement!

How can you make investments in a SIPP?

There are three options:

Transfer from an existing pension

- You can move your current pension pot from your existing pension provider to a new SIPP. Many investors don't realise that pension providers are legally required to follow your instructions and pay the transfer value of your pension, in cash, to your new scheme. Typically it takes around six weeks to set up a new scheme and get your existing pension money transferred.

- If your pension is held in an existing SIPP, it may have restrictive rules which do not allow you to invest in the assets of your choice. In this case, you may be able to liquidate your existing assets and transfer the cash to a new SIPP that is more flexible.

Change assets within existing SIPP

- If you are already invested in a SIPP but are not happy with the investments chosen, you may be able to liquidate your existing assets into cash and then reinvest.

New contributions

- You can start a new SIPP with cash contributions – either a lump sum or monthly payments. If you are considering starting a pension or adding to an existing one, this can be within a new SIPP.

I am often asked if it is difficult to transfer your personal pension into a SIPP. The answer, quite simply, is that it is no more difficult than changing your car insurance. There are costs involved, but these are usually much lower than the cripplingly high costs and fees that many existing pension schemes charge! Combined with the potential for improved performance, the costs are rarely an issue.

What types of pension can you transfer to a SIPP?

✓ Personal and stakeholder pensions and other SIPPs;

✓ Retirement annuity contracts, FSAVCs and most AVCs;

✓ Protected rights pensions accumulated from contracting out of the State Second Pension;

✓ Pensions in income drawdown;

✓ Most 'frozen' pensions that are no longer active.

What investments can you place in your SIPP?

Probably the single biggest benefit of a SIPP is the opportunity to select from a far wider range of investment choices than with a traditional pension. This ability to choose can have a dramatic impact on investment performance, as I shall shortly show.

But, first, exactly what investment choices can you make within a SIPP wrapper? Take a look at the table on the next page:

WHAT INVESTMENTS CAN I CHOOSE?	SIPP	PERSONAL PENSION
Stocks and shares		
Individual UK equities	✔	✗
Overseas equities	✔	✗
UK gilts	✔	✗
Corporate bonds	✔	✗
Futures and options	✔	✗
Investment funds		
Unit trusts	✔	✗
Investment trusts	✔	✗
Open-ended investment companies (OEICs)	✔	✗
Exchange traded funds	✔	✗
Insurance company managed funds	✔	✔
Other investments		
Cash and deposits	✔	✔
Loans	✔	✗
Traded endowment plans	✔	✗
Commercial property and land	✔	✗

Of the 14 asset classes listed above, only TWO are available for personal pension investment. Within a SIPP, however, all of them are available!

For many investors, the whole idea of making sensible investment choices from such a wide variety of possibilities is daunting. How on earth can you be an expert across such a wide range of choices? In fact, how can even an Independent Financial Advisor (IFA) be an expert with such a selection?

The reality is that you can't, and neither can they.

Given this, you need some guidelines about how to approach investment choices. This is exactly what the next chapter investigates. Remember that any investment should be held for the long term, as they can fall as well as rise in value. This means you could get back less than you invested.

Is a SIPP the right option for you?

SIPPs are not for everyone. If you are fortunate enough to be in a defined benefit pension scheme, then it is less likely that a SIPP will offer a better option (although they sometimes will!).

Once you have read the next chapter on the 'perfect' pension, you will see that my recommendations are for assets that are only available either within a SIPP or outside a pension wrapper altogether. If you agree with my analysis, then the SIPP option becomes clearly more attractive than a personal pension – unless your existing pension provides benefits that can't be matched.

Overall, escaping from mediocre fund performance, reducing excessive fees and having the option to invest in better performing assets are the main three reasons to switch to a SIPP.

They are also the main reasons to invest outside a pension plan, as we have previously discussed.

Generally speaking, the benefits of a SIPP increase with the size of your pension pot and the size of your contributions. A stakeholder pension can be a cheaper and better option for investors with very limited resources. Alternatively, a low cost SIPP that still gives you access to a wide variety of fund managers is another option.

If you already have a personal or stakeholder pension, the first and most crucial step is to commission a pension review. This review will show you:

- The current state of your pension;
- Historic performance;
- Level of charges and fees;
- Anticipated pension on retirement;
- Alternative options.

The pension review will be conducted by a regulated IFA who is authorised to provide financial advice.

If you have a defined benefit or final salary scheme, it may be necessary to commission an independent pension report from a pension specialist as the issues are more complex.

Switching your existing pension or changing your investment strategy is an important and far reaching decision. If you have any doubts about the suitability of a SIPP for your circumstances, you should seek professional advice.

Why your IFA may not be your best friend!

And now, a final word about IFAs. If your investments are fairly limited, you may not have a personal relationship with an IFA. But if you have invested in a variety of financial products – maybe including pensions, life assurance, unit trusts and so on – it is highly likely that you have an IFA who has a close relationship with you. They may be a trusted advisor of many years standing.

But, here's the problem. If you talk to your IFA about switching your pension to a SIPP, particularly one that is going to invest in assets such as commercial property, you present them with a number of problems:

1 They will lose the on-going fees they receive from your current pension provider and may even have fees already paid to them 'clawed back'.

2 They are regulated by the Financial Services Authority (FSA), which has established guidelines on how a typical investment portfolio should be made up. For example, they recommend a maximum of 15 per cent of your portfolio in commercial property. If your pension pot is worth, say, £80,000, then 15 per cent of that is £12,000. It is completely impracticable to invest so little in this asset class.

3 The FSA frowns on the inclusion of unregulated investments in a portfolio. Property is unregulated – including the purchase of the very property you live in!

Taking all this together, most IFAs – in my experience – will strongly advise you NOT to switch your pension. And not to invest in unregulated investments. And not to invest more than 15 per cent of your portfolio in commercial property.

They will almost never recommend the radically different approach to investing that I discuss in the next chapter. If you agree with my analysis, you are going to have to take a robust approach to dealing with your IFA!

This goes to the heart of my view that the financial services industry does not have the right approach to giving **you** the best possible advice across the wide variety of investments that are available. Rant over!

Summary

- SIPPs are the 21st century model for a pension;
- You can take full control;
- There is a very wide range of investment possibilities, enabling you to radically improve performance;
- The most important decision is to move your fund from existing underperforming or frozen pensions into a new SIPP;
- There are some pensions, specifically defined benefit pensions, which require a detailed professional report before you give up valuable benefits.

Chapter 7

How to build the 'perfect' pension

I've taken a detailed look at exactly why the existing pensions system is a disaster. Now, it's time to turn to the positives: building a future so that retirement is a joy!

There are some headline issues that the present pensions' mess has highlighted as real problems we don't want to repeat. I will focus on the four key points that need special attention:

Capital preservation – Many existing pension savers have been losing capital and going backwards, even over a 10-15 year period. We want to avoid that at all costs; therefore, risk management is a key factor.

Performance – You need to achieve far higher annualised returns from income and growth in order to have any chance of building the pension pot that you need or generating the income you want in retirement.

Inflation – You need to achieve capital growth and income growth over time to inflation-proof your retirement fund.

Inheritance – You need to do everything possible to avoid losing the value of your assets on death, and be able to pass them on to your inheritors. This rules out the annuity route for most retirees, and even opens the prospect of investing outside the pension system for many people.

Achieving these four objectives comes down to two simple things:

The savings structure – Are you going to save within or outside the pension system? If within the system, then a SIPP offers the best possible flexibility. Outside the pension system, you can choose any structure you like.

Asset choice – This is the critical element that will determine whether or not improvements are delivered to the existing pension schemes in which you may be currently invested.

So, it's time to analyse the characteristics of assets that you would ideally like to hold within your perfect pension. Of course, it is unlikely that any one asset will tick all these boxes, but the more criteria that are satisfied, the better.

All these characteristics are, in my view, right for an asset that is a long-term hold. A completely different set of characteristics would be appropriate for an asset that is being traded in the short term. But, for a pension that is designed to take care of your financial security for the rest of your life, the most important consideration for most of your portfolio should be the long-term view.

As I discussed at the beginning, there are two stages to developing your pension. The first is the building of a pension pot, through capital growth and accumulated income. The second phase is after you retire, when you want to maximise your monthly income.

The most important factors for each stage do vary, although there is also a lot of overlap. To help your understanding, I will discuss each characteristic under the stage in which it fits most appropriately.

Here's a list of the 11 most important characteristics we will discuss:

Stage One: Prior to retirement – Building capital

- Intrinsic value in the asset;
- Low volatility;
- Growth in capital and income over time;

- Excellent returns – Growth;
- Excellent returns – Income;
- Leverage;
- Market timing and value investing.

Stage Two: After retirement - Generating income

- Decoupling of the income stream from the asset price;
- Assured income;
- Defined exit strategy;
- Low risk.

Stage One: Prior to retirement - Building capital

Intrinsic value in the asset

I personally favour assets that have an intrinsic value. The very best is land, and bricks and mortar. At the opposite of the spectrum are shares in a company that is knowledge-based or service-focused. Where is the intrinsic value in that?

All too often, we see companies go bust – regardless of size – and their share value becomes precisely zero. Does this ever happen to a house? Absolutely not.

Low volatility

If your asset drops 70 per cent in value over a short time, it has to grow again by roughly 250 per cent to get back to where it was before. So, the greater the volatility of an asset, the more risk you have of a poor performance in the future. For me, this was illustrated dramatically in the recent UK property and banking crash.

My father, who is an incredibly cautious investor, had most of his portfolio invested in shares – bank shares to be precise. When the bank crisis hit, his portfolio dropped 70 per cent in value overnight. Some three years later, it still isn't back to where it was.

My portfolio is invested in rental property. On average, UK property values dropped 17 per cent from peak pricing. To get back to their former level, only a 21 per cent price recovery was needed, which has almost happened now. Property, generally, has very low volatility compared to share investments.

Growth in capital and income over time

When you place money into a savings account, you get interest every year: that's the income element. However, you get no growth in capital value, so your asset effectively loses value in real terms because of the impact of inflation.

Maybe you invest in gold or other commodities. These provide potential capital growth (although highly volatile) but no income. So, your future is dependent on the vagaries of the market and the economic laws of supply and demand.

Perhaps the very worst investment, within this context, is the annuity that pension savers traditionally purchase. At the time you buy it, you guarantee yourself 100 per cent that there is no capital growth – in fact you now have no capital at all – and you mostly have a fixed income for ever. Hmm, time to rethink, I believe.

Alternatively, an investment in assets such as property means that there will be a significant benefit from growth in both capital and income over time. In general, the income growth will keep pace with inflation and the capital growth is an extra bonus for your heirs, or if you are building your capital before retirement.

Excellent returns - Growth

I have said many times that the key to a better pension is improving performance. But this is where the traditional baskets of shares, gilts and cash have failed miserably.

Let's review: Barclays Capital recently reviewed the performance of the major asset classes for the decade from 2000 to 2010. I'd say that ten years is a reasonable stretch of time for any asset to perform.

The very worst performing was a basket of shares, which came in overall at -14 per cent over the ten year period. In other words, your share portfolio would be worth LESS after ten years of investment.

Gold and oil were listed at first and second place.

In third place was property – a gain of **106 per cent** over ten years, a time period which included the property crash. However, Barclays made one major mistake with the table by failing to include the benefit of leverage, which makes one of the key distinctions for property.

If you include the ability to borrow to fund property, then the overall return jumps to **432 per cent** over ten years and puts property way ahead of **ALL** other asset classes.

Excellent returns - Income

If you are pre-retirement, your retirement fund is going to consist of both capital growth and accumulated income. If you are about to enter retirement, then the income you can generate is paramount. Either way, income is a critical part of how your pension is performing.

So, what is an excellent income? If you have grown up within our 'traditional' financial model, and one that reflects the bank's base rate, right now you probably expect to generate around 2-4 per cent per annum on your savings – or maybe not even that!

And, if you own a portfolio of shares, then the average dividend yield across the FTSE 100 leading shares was just 3.86 per cent per annum, at the time of writing.

I, for one, don't consider that return excellent. For your perfect pension, I would say that income of approaching 10 per cent per annum is excellent. Is this genuinely achievable? You bet. Right now, some investors are benefiting from a range of property-backed investments that offer between seven and 25 per cent net income, per annum. Furthermore, most of these incomes are guaranteed.

To understand the impact of a better annual return, let's see what can happen to a starting sum of just £10,000. I will assume that the income will be reinvested for either a 15-year or a 30-year term, without factoring in the impact of capital growth.

	CAPITAL VALUE AFTER 15 YEARS	CAPITAL VALUE AFTER 30 YEARS
TYPICAL INVESTMENTS		
£10,000 at 2% a year	£13,459	£18,114
£10,000 at 4% a year	£18,009	£32,434
PROPERTY BACKED INVESTMENTS		
£10,000 at 7% a year	£27,590	£76,123
£10,000 at 12% a year	£54,736	£299,599
£10,000 at 20% a year	£154,070	£2,373,763 (yes really!)

This table should help to focus your mind on getting better returns for your investments and to stop believing that pathetic returns of two to five per cent are the norm. How do you think that rich people got rich? By doing what the masses do, or by making smart decisions about their investments?

Leverage

Let's say that you have £25,000 to invest. Generally speaking, the purchase of most asset classes will require a 100 per cent payment with your own money. With property (with a few exceptions), you can borrow to enable a bigger investment to happen.

Typically with UK residential property, you can borrow up to around 75 per cent of the lower of property value or purchase price.

And, if you have decided to switch your existing pension to a SIPP, you can borrow up to 50 per cent of the value of the SIPP to invest in property-related assets (provided that the lender is agreeable).

So, what difference does this make? It can be enormous. Let's compare identical returns, in growth and income from a share portfolio and a property portfolio, assuming you hold both for 20 years.

	SHARE PORTFOLIO	PROPERTY
Value of purchase	£100,000	£100,000
Borrowing taken	Nil	£75,000
Income over 20 years at 5% pa	£100,000	£100,000
Interest paid over 20 years @ 4% pa	Nil	£60,000
Net income received	£100,000	£40,000
Value after 20 years at 5% growth	£265,333	£265,333

	SHARE PORTFOLIO	PROPERTY
Capital profit	£165,333	£165,333
Total profit - net income plus capital growth	£265,333	£205,333
Amount invested	£100,000	£25,000
Return on capital	265%	821%

This shows, in the starkest terms possible, the colossal impact of leverage and why, in many cases, it can help to generate substantially higher returns that, over an extended period, can revolutionise your retirement plans.

Market timing and value investing

All assets that are traded, either on a short term or a long term basis, vary in price across the economic market cycle. It is clearly better to purchase assets around the bottom of a cycle and then benefit, not just from general economic growth, but the upswing in the cycle when prices recover.

The greater the swings in the cycle, the higher the potential growth in years to come.

However, life is a bit more complicated than this. The reasons why the values of assets change are very complex and dependent on far more than economic output alone. For example, shortage of supply can provide an additional price impetus. The availability of finance that restricts or enables purchase is another factor.

My strategy is to combine three factors into your asset purchase. Together, they can offer a far more powerful vehicle for growth in the medium term than any one element alone. These three factors are:

- Invest at the bottom of the cycle, when prices are lowest;
- Buy below the market value of the asset (possible with property but not with shares);
- Buy in a market that is driven by shortage of supply and other distortions that will positively impact the future price growth.

Combine these factors and you have a reduced risk of minimum growth and delivered maximum potential returns!

Stage Two: After retirement - Generating income

Decoupling the income stream from the asset price

For me, this is one of the most important issues to consider when making investments for your long-term pension. Is the income from your asset decoupled from the value of the asset?

Let's take two scenarios. First off, you buy shares in a large manufacturing company. You are looking for an increased price over time, and also a regular stream of dividends. However, the company share price falls. Why? Because the prospects for the business are perceived as not being so good. This usually reflects the real world situation. So, what does the company do? It reduces the dividend to reflect the poorer performance and to conserve cash.

In this way, the share price is very much linked to the income you receive.

In contrast, take a rental property investment opportunity. Because of market conditions, the value of the property falls. Since you don't plan to trade the asset anytime soon, this is a theoretical fall in value that has absolutely no meaning unless you plan to sell.

But what's happened to the rental income? Absolutely nothing. It carries on, just as before. In fact, in both the UK and many other overseas countries, the lack of buyers has resulted in an increase in renters and actually **improved** the income stream.

In this way, the capital value is decoupled from the income stream, which continues regardless. This is a great characteristic to have for any asset you purchase for a pension.

Assured income

For most people after retirement, the monthly income becomes paramount. It's what you will rely on to cover your living expenses and enable you to do the things you always dreamed of doing.

So, having a guaranteed income stream is a great benefit. That's one reason why many people have savings accounts. Their capital might not be protected (at least, not against inflation), the income might be rubbish, but at least it is certain that it will be received.

Well, I think you should demand MORE. There are many assets that can offer an assured income over periods ranging typically from three to ten years – and at a much higher level than you would expect from savings accounts or government gilts.

What assured income is possible? At the time of writing, the options vary between around seven per cent and 20 per cent net of costs and charges.

Defined exit strategy

One of the few benefits of holding a portfolio of quoted shares is that they are generally easy to buy and sell in the market. This means that switching can be done quickly if you believe that there are better options. Many other assets – such as property – while beneficial in many ways, are not so quickly or easily sold. If you want to change your portfolio, it can take considerable time and cost a large amount.

One way to get the best of both worlds is to invest in assets that offer a defined exit strategy. These are constructed in such a way that the investor has, at pre-determined times, the opportunity to sell the asset at a price based on a pre-agreed formula back to the vendor.

Some schemes, for example, have assets that can be bought back at three-, five- and ten-year intervals. The guaranteed price ranges from the price paid, to 150 per cent of the price paid, to 80 per cent of the current valuation at the time of sale.

The beauty of having such a defined exit strategy is that you don't have to take it, but it does increase your options and gives you certainty that – at a minimum – your capital is protected. It also means that you can switch into other assets without any great drama.

Low risk

I could write an entire book around the subject of risk and risk management. Frankly, when your retirement is at stake, I'm not a believer in taking risks with your money. So, how is it, when every IFA in the world tells you to be cautious, they continue to recommend a basket of various company shares as the foundation for your pension – even though the value of shares in the UK today is no higher than it was in 1997, some 15 years ago! And, that's before the impact of inflation.

I believe that this approach is monstrous and it entirely misunderstands the nature of risk. In the context of investment, the Oxford English Dictionary defines risk as: "the possibility of financial loss." This is exactly what has happened to everyone whose money has been invested in a basket of UK shares for the last 15 years.

In fact, we should consider risk at each stage of the development of our pension. If you are at the first stage – building your capital – and you have more than 20 years until you retire, then you can afford to take a bigger risk than if you have already retired and are now reliant on a monthly income. At this latter point, you really can't afford to take substantial risks, either with your capital or your income.

For some people, this may mean switching assets at the time of retirement to change the risk profile of their portfolio. In point of fact, within traditional pensions, it's very normal to adjust the balance between shares, gilts and cash as pension age approaches.

With other asset choices, this switch may not be desirable or financially viable; I will come back to this question later.

Perversely, if you have left your pension provision until later in life and you have a short time to go to retirement – say, less than 15 years – you are going to need an aggressive growth strategy to build an acceptable pension pot in time. While, in theory, you should be taking less risks than ever, you may face the situation where the only option to successfully build the pension you need is to accept a higher level of risk in return for a potentially high return.

If your strategy goes wrong – and that is always possible – then your portfolio may not deliver what you want. What is absolutely guaranteed, however, is that if you don't follow this path, then there is a 100 per cent certainty that you will fail to achieve your goals!

In my opinion, risk means understanding, and taking advantage of, these six criteria:

- Pricing based on intrinsic value and not market sentiment;

- Truly limited supply and fundamental demand from basic human needs;
- Picking the right time in the economic cycle;
- Investing in assets with low volatility;
- Assets that decouple capital growth from income;
- Assets that provide both capital growth and income growth.

If you measure the 'traditional' investments of shares, gilts and cash savings against the above criteria, all of them fall woefully short. In my view, these traditional investments are worse than risky; they vary between a guarantee of non-performance and the highly likely outcome that you will lose money!

You have to do better than this – much better. The good news is that, thankfully, you can!

Summary

There are four key elements to building a perfect pension: capital preservation, performance, protection from inflation and transferring the fund on death;

There are 11 key characteristics of a perfect pension. Seven that are relevant when building the fund, four that are critical when taking income;

Fortunately, there are assets which fit these characteristics, but they are a world away from the traditional pension choices of shares, gilts and cash!

Chapter 8

Exploding the myths about portfolio management

A lot of time and attention is given by the press and the financial services industry to the ongoing discussion about the kind of portfolio you should hold at particular stages of your financial career. The debate centres on not just how the portfolio should be split between the three main asset classes of traditional pension investments (shares, gilts and cash), but exactly what shares should be included in the basket.

You will no doubt have heard the common myth that says that the more actively traded your portfolio is, the more money you will make. What is certain about this is that your advisors will make more money, because 'churning' a portfolio generates fees with every sale and purchase!

What is far less certain is whether you benefit from it.

Let's look at a realistic example. Take a 15-year period and consider an investment in a basket of shares. For argument's sake, I'll choose the shares that make up the FTSE 100 index – this consists of the UK's largest companies which are supposed to have low volatility and steady growth. Fifteen years ago, the FTSE index was 4604; today it is 5260. This is an annualised 0.85 per cent growth over that entire period. The inclusion of a wide variety of shares did not stop the appalling performance – and any of these FTSE 100 shares will be selected for **your** pension portfolio!

So, selecting a portfolio of shares doesn't stop poor performance. Surely your IFA can do better than this by selecting portfolios that perform better and meet your needs more closely?

In January 2011, the FSA issued a discussion paper about portfolio selection that came to the following conclusion:

"The high number of unsuitable investment selections we see in the pensions and investment markets is still a significant concern…

"Of the investment files assessed as unsuitable between March 2008 and September 2010, we rated half of these as unsuitable on the grounds that the investment selection failed to meet the risk a customer is willing and able to take.

"Even where the risk profile of the customer is correctly assessed, the product or portfolio (and underlying asset-allocation) does not always match this profile. This can be due to a failure to select investments that match the risk a customer is willing and able to take, or a failure to take account of all aspects of a customer's investment objectives and financial situation."

Between the abysmal market performance and the serious problems that the FSA identified in the recommendations that IFAs are making, what chance do you have in building a strong pension?

My view of portfolio selection is radically different. Firstly, I would pick different assets – namely, those that meet my criteria as I discussed above. These assets, by their very nature, will require larger amounts of money for investment; therefore, many portfolios may only contain one or two of them.

These assets, held over the long term, will produce rising income and capital growth. For me, one major factor is to look at the typical market cycle and make sure, wherever possible, that I invest for two or more cycles.

Let's take property as an example. Since the Second World War, the UK property cycle has averaged at ten years; two cycles last for 20 years. Let's assume we invest around the bottom of a cycle and also below market value. Do you have any doubts you are going to see substantial capital growth?

Here's how it looks:

Property value at start	£100,000
Purchase price (20% below market value)	£80,000
Value after 20 years (at 5% growth pa)	£265,000
Profit	£185,000
Return on investment	230%

And this return is without factoring in the benefit of leverage, or the net income received over the period, both of which make further positive differences to your overall profit.

Higher risk asset allocation

While I would recommend that most of your pension is invested in low-risk assets, I believe there is also scope for limited investment in higher risk assets in these three scenarios:

Using the leftover cash in your pension pot

Let's suppose you have a current pension pot that is worth £80,000. You decide to liquidate it, turn it into cash and place it in a SIPP for investment in assets that promise higher returns. You invest in a property that requires £65,000. This leaves £15,000 in cash in your SIPP, which is not going to generate more than, say, three per cent a year in savings.

There is a strong argument for using this final amount for a higher risk investment, maybe in alternative investments of some kind.

Reinvesting your accrued income

Now, let's say your new investment strategy is generating £12,000 a year in income that is being accumulated in your pension pot. In itself, £12,000 will not be enough to purchase, for example, another property. But leaving it as cash or savings is not helping to 'sweat' your assets. So again, careful investment in a higher risk proposition could be a better approach.

New savings

You have invested the bulk of your pension pot into safe, low-risk but high-performance assets that meet my criteria. You continue to save for your pension on a monthly or quarterly basis. These savings are not enough to purchase a major asset, but form a useful additional sum that can also work hard for you.

Once more, choosing a higher risk and higher return investment might be a good investment balance.

As a rule of thumb, I'd say that 80 per cent of your portfolio should be in low-risk assets that, nevertheless, offer extremely attractive returns and both capital and income growth. I'd also suggest that up to 20 per cent should be invested in high risk/higher return investments that can provide an added bonus without risking the overall portfolio.

Why your IFA will never agree!

This approach to portfolio management is my own personal view. Although I am a Chartered Accountant, this is not professional advice. What's more, my approach is completely contrary to established opinion! I make no apology for this. My belief is that 'established opinion' has resulted in the pensions' disaster that most people now face. Moreover, the causes of this calamity are clearly to be found in the current structure of the financial services industry.

Let's suppose you have decided to:

- Switch your existing personal pension into a SIPP that you control;
- Invest it primarily in property-related assets – with only one investment making up the bulk of your portfolio;
- This necessitates investing in non-regulated assets (all property is non-regulated, including the purchase of your own house or flat!);
- Invest up to 20 per cent of your pension pot in higher risk/higher return assets;
- Wave goodbye to shares, gilts and cash investments.

What will your IFA say?

My view is that most IFAs will have very little to say – they will be speechless. You have broken every 'rule' they have been trained to follow. What's more, you have gone against the 'guidance' of the FSA (which, as an IFA, you ignore at your own peril).

It gets worse. You have undermined your IFA's entire understanding of portfolio theory. And last (but certainly not least), you have hit them in their pocket since they will no longer receive annual income as part of their fee for recommending your disastrous pension!

If I were you, I wouldn't bother asking for their opinion; you already know their answer.

Summary

Traditional portfolio management no longer works in the new world of property investment;

It's a fallacy to assume that better performance comes from a balanced portfolio – that only arose because of huge volatility in the underlying asset (shares);

The Financial Services Authority recently found that up to 50 per cent of IFAs were giving wrong advice; so much for the experts!

It still makes sense to take a higher risk approach with a small part of your portfolio, maybe up to 20 per cent. This can be used to invest in products that have lower cash requirements, enabling you to fully invest your cash in your SIPP, and also re-invest your income each year in higher performing assets;

Don't ask your IFA for their opinion, unless you want a guaranteed negative response!

Chapter 9

Your secret weapon - The right asset selection

The single biggest factor to helping you improve the performance of your pension is getting your selection of assets correct. That is why this chapter is of the utmost importance.

It's at this stage that I should declare a personal bias and explain a little about my background. I have a very clear view of what assets I believe should be held for retirement – whether it is inside or outside a pension wrapper. It's important for you to understand how I arrived at these conclusions.

I started my professional career as a Chartered Accountant with one of the 'big six' firms in the City of London. What that gave me was great experience in understanding the fine details of finance and economics. It also made me cautious about taking risks.

I also come from a family of entrepreneurs who have never been afraid to run their own businesses and make tough decisions. Over the last 30 years, my own businesses have included retail, wholesale, publishing and consultancy.

Whatever 'other' businesses I ran, underneath it all was a continuing investment in, and involvement with, property. In 1982, I purchased my first commercial property. For eight years, I ran a property development company in London with my brother, who is an architect. And since 2005, I've run Axis Property Investment – a company that specialises in the acquisition of investment property for investor clients, with a particular emphasis on long-term investment for retirement.

You could say that my entire family is in the property business.

My mother is fully invested in commercial property (retail shops);

My first brother lives in the USA and builds real estate and holds a rental portfolio;

My second brother is an architect, property developer and investor in a range of property assets, including commercial (shops and offices), residential and ground rents;

My third brother lives off the income from a residential portfolio.

All my own personal assets are invested in property, including commercial (office, shops and hotel rooms) and a broad residential portfolio of houses and flats, both in the UK and internationally.

In 2002, I wrote the first major course to help people get started in property investment called 'PIPS' – the Property Investment Profit System – and I continue to run investment workshops and seminars across the UK.

You will have noticed that, throughout this book, I have been dropping little hints regarding property investments. Now, it should come as no surprise to you that my generic recommendation for your retirement (and a **strong** recommendation) is that the majority of your retirement portfolio be invested in various property assets.

But, why have I come to this conclusion? Let me briefly reveal the four strands of my reasoning:

Strand One - Logic and analysis

In the previous chapter, I listed 11 characteristics that would be present in a 'perfect' pension. Here is the list again:

Stage One: Prior to retirement – Building capital

- Intrinsic value in the asset;

- Low volatility;
- Growth in capital and income over time;
- Excellent returns – Growth;
- Excellent returns – Income;
- Leverage;
- Market timing and value investing.

Stage Two: After retirement - Generating income

- Decoupling of the income stream from the asset price;
- Assured income;
- Defined exit strategy;
- Low risk.

I have already discussed each of these characteristics in detail. If you review property-related assets against these factors, you will find that most of them are fulfilled. However, if you review the 'big three' traditional investments of shares, gilts and cash against these factors, you will find most of them are sorely lacking.

Strand Two - My own experience

I practice what I preach. I can say with absolute certainty that, as the years pass, my property portfolio grows in income and value. Sure, it has ups and downs and I've certainly made a few mistakes. But, taken together, the passing of time has unquestionably shown me that my property portfolio is headed where it needs it to be.

Beyond this, the experience of my friends, colleagues and clients confirms the same conclusion. Look around you at the people who are truly wealthy. You will find that a high proportion of them have invested heavily in property. I interviewed 12 very rich property investors for my PIPS course. Every one of them started with nothing; one began as a car mechanic, another is an architectural draughtsman who left school at 15 and went to his first job with holes in the soles of his shoes.

Today, all of them have **six-figure incomes** from rents. Some even have incomes in excess of £1m a year!

Strand Three – My position within Axis Property Investment

Today, I live my life within the property sector. Sure, you could say that doesn't make me an expert in other investments and that's true. But I comment on what I see, not on what I don't see. And what I see are hundreds of clients making great investment choices and owning assets – both inside and outside pension wrappers – that will provide the returns they need for retirement. I'm fortunate to have such a close day-by-day connection with the facts that I am sharing here.

Strand Four - Market timing

My personal investments in property have been made at all points of the market cycle, including 2006 and 2007 when UK property was at its peak pricing. Of course, I helped myself by buying below market value. The point is that, when you invest for the long term and you expect to hold assets for at least TWO market cycles, the precise point of entry is less important.

Notice that I didn't say 'not important'. That's because, if you can get the timing right and invest around the bottom of the cycle, you will gain some added benefits:

- Shorter time to capital growth;
- Steeper growth curve;
- Increased rental yields;
- Even lower risk.

The good news is the publication of this book in 2012 coincides with the absolutely perfect time to hit the bottom of the cycle – both with UK property and other international markets, such as the USA. From a timing perspective, this is the best opportunity in a generation to invest at rock-bottom prices. I need to be completely clear about this: you miss the timing of this investment opportunity at your peril. You will not see the same low pricing again during your lifetime.

When you add together the four strands of my argument for retirement investing in property-related assets, I hope you come to the same conclusion that I reached many years ago. What's more, the current timing of the property cycle adds even more urgency to the issue.

Exactly what property-related assets can I invest in?

At this point, I need to distinguish between assets that can be invested inside a SIPP wrapper –therefore benefiting from tax relief (but with other restrictions) – and property assets that can be invested outside a SIPP wrapper.

Property assets outside a pension wrapper

The great news is that there are no restrictions at all outside a pension wrapper; you can invest in exactly what you like. You can leverage your asset by borrowing as much as is possible without restriction. And, you can buy and sell as you wish.

Beyond this, you can decide on any ownership structure you prefer, such as giving all or part of the asset to family members, and so on.

The largest segment of property assets that can be purchased outside a pension wrapper but not inside (according to current legislation) is residential property. A simple definition of residential property is living accommodation that includes a kitchen of any kind.

Normal buy-to-let property, houses and flats, is considered residential property. Therefore, the pension wrapper is excluded from a major part of property investment.

Of course, a huge amount of property investment involves residential property – and some of it offers exceptional returns. At the time of writing, as one example, Axis Property Investment has UK residential property that offers 10 per cent net income with a five-year guaranteed contract. Similarly, in the USA, net incomes up to 20 per cent per annum are achievable.

However, none of these property investments can be placed within a pension wrapper.

The second major group of property assets that have to be held outside a pension wrapper are those assets that could qualify within the rules as a SIPP product, but the vendor has decided that they don't need to go to the expense of getting them approved.

A current example of such assets is hotel rooms in the USA, where you can receive a four-year guaranteed income at 25 per cent per annum net. However, because these investments are available to people worldwide, the developer feels no need to make special arrangements to meet the SIPP requirements for UK investors.

These are clear and unambiguous examples of some great investments with high, guaranteed returns – but they are only available outside a pension wrapper.

Moving on, I want to discuss the property-related assets that can be held inside the new SIPP pension wrapper. Remember, each of these assets can also be held personally, it is your choice whether to include them within a SIPP. Take a look at Chapter Six for the discussion on whether to hold an asset personally or within a SIPP.

Property assets inside a pension wrapper (SIPP only)

The pension rules define what can be held within a SIPP. Bear in mind that, just because the asset can qualify for a SIPP, this does **NOT** mean that the vendor will always choose to do the extensive work needed to get the asset approved. Only approved assets can be held within your SIPP.

Regulated and unregulated assets

There are categories of assets that the FSA regulates and assets that it does not. Property and land are not regulated assets. This can cause confusion because the SIPP wrapper (think of it as a container) is a regulated product.

This means that you have to separate the creation of your new SIPP (an asset container) – which is a regulated process involving a licensed IFA – from your investment in non-regulated assets, which you can now place in your SIPP.

This also means most IFAs will actively try to dissuade you from investing in property because it is a non-regulated asset the FSA frowns on as an investment choice. You can be sure IFAs will particularly dislike the fact property is likely make up the bulk of your portfolio.

One IFA told me that he could never recommend any property asset unless it made up less than four per cent of a portfolio. Since the average pension pot is less than £100,000, the four per cent rule would be no investment higher than £4,000 - clearly impossible with property related assets!

So, let's take a look at what the rules make allowable for investment within a SIPP. It's important to know that there is no restriction on location, so the property can be anywhere in the world – provided that the SIPP approval process has been followed within the UK.

Allowable investments - Commercial property

- Retail shops;
- Factories & Warehouses
- Offices;
- Hotel rooms & resort property;
- Student accommodation;
- Care homes;
- Self-storage units;
- Car parks;
- No doubt more will be added in the future.

It is also important to note that it's possible to have a variety of ownership structures for the assets listed above. We have seen four different options for investors:

Straight ownership of the assets

This would include the straightforward leasehold or freehold ownership of a hotel room or ownership of an office unit.

Bonds

Effectively, bonds are a loan to the vendor, secured on the asset. Bonds lend themselves to more modest levels of investment and often carry fixed returns.

Fractional ownership

This is where ownership of a room is split into parts – maybe 12 parts – and each one carries a separate ownership deed. This works well with highly priced resort properties where individual investors can rarely afford the complete property. An example of a fractional ownership is a holiday villa in the Caribbean where the unit price is more than £1m. However, fractionals may also be available from around £100,000.

Share ownership

This is option where the asset is owned through a corporate structure by investors. Each share gives you – the investor – certain rights. Shares can be bought and sold independently of the underlying asset. This has clear advantages in certain situations, particularly where there is a real possibility of the entire asset being sold for a profit later on.

Allowable investments - Land

- Farmland and Forestry - including teak/bamboo/green oil plantations.
- Graveyard plots;
- Development land;

Land that is being used productively provides investors with the benefit of both income and capital growth over time. This is different to development land that has no income, but a potentially high capital gain if, for example, planning consent for a change of use is obtained.

Now for a word of warning: the UK has a number of companies that offer so-called 'development land', where they anticipate the gaining of planning consent to turn farmland into residential building land. History repeatedly shows that this almost never happens; most investors are locked into overpriced farmland with no prospect of either selling their 'asset' or achieving a capital gain. Buyer beware!

Allowable investments – Loans

These can include loans to various property investment companies, such as property developers, hotel construction companies, and more.

The inclusion of loans as an allowable asset class within SIPPS has opened up a raft of creative approaches to funding various property investment ventures.

What should you choose?

With such a wealth of opportunity to invest your SIPP fund, you really are spoilt for choice. At the same time, you can hardly become an expert across all these possibilities overnight – if indeed at all.

I would strongly recommend that you get specialist advice from people who know the property investment and SIPP markets. Whoever you chose to go to, the most important point is that you don't go blindly into selecting investments for your SIPP, but you take advice – and quickly!

Summary

- The right asset allocation is of the utmost importance in achieving better performance;
- My advice is to throw out the 'old' investment model of shares, gilts and cash – it's failed;
- Bring in the new investment model (not so new for many multi-millionaire investors) of property and related assets;
- Use market timing to invest at the bottom of the property cycle – perfect right now;
- Work with experts who know and understand the market, so that you don't have to learn everything yourself. Most investors just don't have the time.

Chapter 10

Property investment made easy

If you are like many people saving for a pension, you started with a plan many years ago and left it to your pension company to decide everything about investment. This means that you are likely to have no investment experience at all. Or, perhaps you did take control of your pension fund and created a SIPP, but chose to invest in shares and government funds.

With little direct experience of property investment, you may feel very nervous and unprepared about placing retirement funds in this asset class. Your concerns may include:

- Which property investments to choose;
- The time you may need (and probably don't have!) to manage your investments; and,
- Taking on risks that you don't even recognise.

Phew! These fears could be enough to put you off investing in property before you even get started. But this would be a big mistake. Look around you at the people who are really wealthy. Almost universally, they either made a lot of their money in property, or chose to invest in property once they had made it.

In this chapter, I'm going to dispel common myths about property investment and explain just how a newcomer to property can made good decisions, minimise the risks, and spend very little time on management. In fact, in some cases, it takes less time than it would to review a share portfolio!

Where are you now?

The key point to keep in mind at all times is that the existing asset classes that traditionally make up retirement planning have **failed**.

To put it bluntly, they have **failed miserably and to a huge degree!** So, when you consider property investment, remember that the choice is either to stay with the 'same old' investments and get the 'same old' rubbish returns, or be willing to step outside your existing experience and do something that can make an enormously positive difference to your future financial security.

Use other people's expertise

I am a great believer in what's called the 'OP Formula'. The 'OP' stands for Other People's. So, if you don't know enough yourself, you rely on Other People's Expertise (OPE). We don't have to know all the answers ourselves, but we do have to know a man who does.

The problem is that many aspiring property investors ask the wrong people, they turn to their family and friends (who don't have any property investments), their IFA (who wants to sell them shares), and so on. Even existing property investors may not have the breadth of experience that covers all the bases; all too frequently, they provide a very narrow view of what they think is a 'good' investment.

My advice is simple: find a company that specialises in working exclusively with property investors and has a wide range of products, a company that has been in the market for years and has a depth of knowledge that provides you with the missing pieces. Discuss your strategy with these specialists and collaboratively work out what would be the best investments for you.

It's difficult to make a bad mistake

That might surprise you. It's true that if you buy the wrong share, you can end up losing your shirt. However, if you work with the right company, it is extremely unlikely you will make a 'bad' investment. In retrospect, I paid a bit too much for a couple of my own properties and that could be considered a mistake, but over the years they have done well.

In property investment, the key is to understand that time heals all errors. Values will rise over time; rents will rise over time. Any loans remain fixed, so **it is inevitable that your equity and profit will increase**. There are few other assets you can say that about.

Use 'System ZERO' to save time

My philosophy in property investment has always been to ensure I spend as little time as possible on my portfolio. So, I invented the concept of 'System ZERO' – that is, to aim to use ZERO of my time and ZERO of my effort by utilising the skills and expertise of others. Basically, it's about structuring the deal so that the OPE Formula kicks in again – with maximum results for your investments. Only this time, it includes Other People's Time (OPT).

Property investors are fortunate people: the whole industry is served by professional property managers who take care of looking after your tenants. Depending on your instructions, you will never know who your tenants are and rarely speak to your property managers – unless it is to authorise a repair or to talk about increasing the rent!

And, if you truly want a totally 'hands-off' investment, you can choose from the growing number of SIPP-compliant commercially focused property deals, such as hotel rooms, student accommodation, care homes and many more. These are fully managed on your behalf and you don't need to think about anything except banking your cheque!

Managing risk

Do you think there is any risk in holding a portfolio of shares? Of course there is – enormous risk – which is why you are looking at alternative investment propositions. This clearly means that risk is relative. Property carries a generally lower level of risk to your capital for five important reasons:

1 The fundamental demand for property to live in;

2 The intrinsic value in the land and the construction costs;

3 The relatively low price volatility over a short time. For example, shares can lose 70 per cent of their value overnight, but property rarely changes in value at more than 15 per cent in a year;

4 Your ability to invest at the bottom of the property cycle – in other words, right NOW!). This is a massive element of risk reduction and is something that happens once every ten to 20 years;

5 The ability to invest in property **below market value**. Work with a good acquisition company and they will use their collective buying power and industry contacts to negotiate very competitive pricing across a range of assets. When was the last time a bank agreed to take £30,000 and then put £40,000 in a deposit account for you?

Taking these five points together, the risk to your capital is, frankly, far less than the risk in share investment. In reality, it is extremely small. Your focus should be on how much capital you are going to generate in the future, not if you are going to generate anything at all!

I have dealt with the issue of risk to your capital, but what about the risk to your income?

Well, what happens when you own shares in a company that is experiencing problems? They usually stop paying – or reduce – the dividend. Your income is absolutely not secure. You can, of course, invest in savings accounts and government bonds, but the interest you receive is so bad it won't even keep up with inflation. As I write this chapter, five-year UK government bonds are showing a yield of 0.8 per cent per annum. That is most certainly not going to provide what you need.

With property, however, you have rental income. The current market is difficult for buyers, which means that even **more** people are renting. In fact, rents have never been stronger. What happens if a tenant stops paying rent? You get rid of them and get another one. By their very nature, rents are robust and relatively risk free.

Some investments – such as hotel rooms, student accommodation and care homes – depend on generating certain levels of occupancy to give you a good return. Part of my company's due diligence is to investigate the projections and decide whether the forecast income is realistically achievable. In order to reach an informed and balanced judgement, we will consider the location, historic occupancy levels for similar accommodation, pricing policy and more. You don't need to be expert in these factors because we already are!

Buy into a system, not a property!

My company is a great believer in end-to-end support for our clients. Whoever you do decide to work with on acquisition, my strong recommendation is that comprehensive support should be included in the service you receive. With this in mind, look for an acquisition company that:

- Sifts and examines investment propositions and rejects those that do not meet strict criteria. This ensures that you only get the best-of-the-best;

- Completes due diligence to reduce the risk to you, the investor;

- Negotiates favourable pricing and terms that would not be available to you individually;
- Makes the purchase process as easy as possible;
- Provides support and advice throughout the process;
- Provides access to all necessary professionals;
- Ensures that effective management of the property is in place.
- The final result is that you should be comfortable. You are receiving benefits that extend further than the property itself. Effectively, you 'buy into' an end-to-end system.

When you do this, you:

- Reduce your need for expertise;
- Reduce your investment of time;
- Access deals and pricing, which you couldn't find or negotiate yourself; and,
- Reduce risks in multiple ways.

Above all else, working with an acquisition company that offers an end-to-end system will transform your ability to invest in property safely and easily.

However, a word of warning: make sure the company you work with has experience in, and offers property for, both SIPP and direct investment. In this book, I have explained carefully why sometimes the correct approach is to invest within a SIPP and why sometimes it isn't. You need a single partner who can deliver for either strategy.

More options for risk-averse investors

Depending on your attitude to risk and the kind of property assets you invest in, you can take rental insurance to cover non-payment. Obviously, this will slightly reduce your income, but it does offer additional peace of mind.

You can also invest in property assets that have **guaranteed income returns**. Such properties can range from long-term lets to housing associations, government-supported programs for asylum seekers, hotel rooms and care homes and much, much more. If you have decided to invest in retirement assets outside a SIPP, then the range of possible guaranteed income property is even greater. At the time of writing, for example, my company could offer investors 25 per cent net income guaranteed for four years, on an investment of £30,000.

These guaranteed returns are sometimes fixed for a defined period, sometimes increasing as the asset matures. A good acquisition company will advise you on the different options.

Guaranteed exit strategies

You may have a clearly defined timescale for exit. Since the future capital value of property can only be forecast, it is possible that – at the time you want to exit – the price available does not match what you expected. This could be because growth is running a little behind your earlier expectations.

In cases where it is really important for you to know exactly when your property investment will mature, there are a number of options that provide a guaranteed exit for investors, with a predetermined formula for the exit price.

These formulas range from a simply guarantee of 100 per cent of your investment back, to an amount that could be between 120 to 150 per cent of your investment returned. It could even be a formula that is linked to an independent valuation at that time. In general, however, the lower the exit price guarantee is, the higher the guaranteed income in the meantime.

Summary

- Property investment, when done correctly, offers potentially high returns combined with low risk.You don't need to be an expert if you use Other People's Expertise (OPE);
- There are ways of reducing the risk even further by selecting investments with guaranteed income and/or guaranteed exit strategies;
- Most property investment will require very little of your time – if you follow the System ZERO principles;
- Working with a company that offers an end-to-end system will benefit you in several clear-cut ways: by saving time, by enabling you to access deals that would otherwise not be available and by reducing risk.

Chapter 11

Retirement the way you want it to be!

Over the course of this book, I've introduced you to the building blocks that you need to develop a radically different pension strategy. There's an enormous amount of information I've presented to you, with two aims in mind: to help you understand why existing pensions are a disaster, and to show you that there are alternatives that can enable you to provide for a happier and more fulfilling retirement – bolstered by more income!

The final, and most important, job for me is to give you a straightforward framework on which to build your new pension structure. This is going to vary from person to person, and it is probably going to need the input of regulated financial advisors.

I have to repeat here that I am not providing individual financial advice – I know nothing about your financial affairs – and so my comments are generic and should not be adopted without professional consideration of you particular circumstances.

Eight steps to a profitable pension

Step One – Complete an audit

Where are you now? What do you already have in place for your pension?

- Existing personal pension(s);
- Frozen personal pension(s) (no longer accepting contributions);
- Existing SIPP(s);
- Other investments outside a pension wrapper, including property;
- Savings accounts including ISAs.

For each of these, you need to check the current value, the investment performance over past few years and the potential income that your investments, collectively, could produce on retirement if you carry on doing what you are doing.

Step Two – Ask for a pension review

Most people with personal pensions, whether current or frozen, don't have the latest information about the value of their pension pot, its recent performance, your anticipated income on retirement, the impact of charges and fees, and much more. For this reason, it is vitally important that you seek a pension review from a reputable organisation that uses a regulated IFA to provide a detailed report of your current policies.

If you have a defined benefit/final salary scheme pension, then you may need a more detailed report from an independent pension specialist, as this may require more analysis and expertise to advise on the best option.

Step Three – Estimate the likely shortfall

Age of retirement?

The age you plan to retire has a huge impact on the level of income that existing investments can provide. Even a few years delay can make a material difference. So, you need to make a plan now, in order to evaluate what will be available to you. What age do you intend to retire – 55, 60, 65, 70, even 75? They are all possible.

In the first chapter, I presented key statistics about survival. If we take the example of a man aged 65, he can expect to survive for 21 years. So, if he retires at 75 he will, on average, reduce his time in retirement by 50 per cent to around ten years. No wonder that incomes at age 75 can be much higher from the same pension pot!

Let's illustrate this with a real-life example. Suppose you initially put £20,000 into a pension when you are 45 and you didn't make any further contributions. Assume your investment has grown at seven per cent a year.

After 20 years, at the age of 65, your pension pot would be worth £77,300. This would buy an annuity of about £4,480 per year, or £373 per month. This is a real example from the highest paying annuity provider at the time of writing.

Now, if you delay your retirement until you are 70, your pension pot grows to £108,500 – some 40 per cent more. Because life expectancy is shorter, annuity rates are more generous. So, your new income would be £7,269 or £605 per month. That's 62 per cent higher as a result of a five-year delay in retirement.

Two levels of income

The second variable is the level of income you wish to have. In my experience, most people have two figures in mind.

The first income figure is based on 'survival'; this is the minimum income that you need to take care of everyday needs - housing, food, clothing, limited travel and so on. This is not what you want, but realise that if you had that amount you could 'get by'.

The second income figure means 'freedom': the freedom to do, within reason, what you choose to do. Whether it is to go where you want, spend time with friends, enjoy the little luxuries that life offers, perhaps take up a new sport or hobby. Not surprisingly, this income figure is very much higher than the one for survival.

Once you know the income you want and the age you want to retire at, you can add up all your various retirement plans and savings – both inside and outside a pension wrapper – and see what the shortfall is.

Having got this far, a lucky few will have **NO** shortfall. If that's you, the pressure is off. You may not have the most efficient and productive investments, but doing better will be a matter of choice, not necessity.

If, on the other hand, you have identified a shortfall, it's time to decide what to do about it.

Step Four – Make the decision about what to do

You are at crunch point. There are two simple choices. You can either continue as you are, maybe throwing more money at your existing underperforming pension, or can you decide to adopt a more proactive approach and take real control over your future.

Since the premise of this entire book is that the current pension system is disastrous, I hope you will agree that it's time to make big changes. But, whether your ultimate decision is to stay with what you already have or adopt a new approach, the most important part of the equation is to do the analysis and come to a decision that is right for you.

If you agree with my analysis of the current pension problems and my suggested solutions, then here are the next steps.

Step Five – Set up your SIPP

If you have an existing personal pension, and you have received an independent pension review or specialist report, the first and most important step is to transfer the cash value of the assets in your pension pot to a new SIPP. This allows you to take control and improve asset selection.

Step Six - Decide on the investment structure

In Chapter Five, I discussed the pros and cons of investing inside or outside a pension wrapper. If you already have a pension that you are switching to a SIPP, then this question does not arise. You can't take assets out of the pension wrapper once they are inside the system. So, your focus will be on investment in assets that are SIPP-compatible.

However, if you are considering investing new funds in assets for your retirement, then you need to question whether the pension wrapper is the best alternative. I hope that Chapter Five gave you a good insight into this, but you may also need professional advice to come to a decision.

Many investors have a strategy that involves multiple options. If, for example, you have reached your limit of pension contributions, then you will have no option but to invest outside a pension. And, if the passing on of your assets is as important as gaining an income in retirement, then holding assets personally might be the way to go.

In that point, I'm reminded of my own mother who is heavily invested in commercial real estate (retail shops). She chose to keep her investments outside a pension wrapper so that her estate could be left to her children and grandchildren. This approach also gives her the maximum flexibility in retirement since she can, if needed, raise capital by either taking a loan or selling one of the properties.

Step Seven - Make your asset selection

At this stage, all that remains for you to do is to choose the right assets for investment. If you agree with my analysis, this will be predominantly – even entirely – in property-related assets and alternative investments.

If you are like most pension savers, you would have previously handed over all responsibility for investment to your pensions company, and now the whole idea of taking control and making investment decisions is scary. For good reason, I might add. After all, how are you suddenly expected to be an expert in selecting one property investment over another? How can you genuinely weigh up the potential risks and rewards in a confident manner?

As a solution to this dilemma, I would strongly suggest you seek a consultation with an adviser who can help you devise a detailed investment strategy. This will enable you to develop a clear understanding about the choices available to you and that fit your requirements for timescale, growth, income and amount of capital investment. You can also discuss which investments best suit a strategy of personal investment as opposed to those within a SIPP wrapper.

When your consultant has helped you weigh up the available options, you can then approach an acquisition partner to help you source alternative investments with potential returns that are way above average.

Step Eight – Complete a periodic review

As with all investments, I recommend that you review your portfolio periodically. If you were invested in a traditional pension, this would normally be done by the pension company on an annual basis. Depending upon its performance, some of your portfolio would be sold and other shares, gilts and so on would be purchased. Changes could also happen as you approach retirement age and the pension company would naturally want to reduce volatility.

In contrast, your portfolio is going to be different. If you hold property assets, many of these will be for life. Other assets will have a defined exit strategy at pre-determined points that will naturally make ideal times for review. In general, though, your portfolio will not need the same detailed attention as a share portfolio. This is a good thing and underlies the longer term, low volatility nature of your new portfolio.

Summary

- Retirement can be the way you want it to be – happy and stress-free!

- Follow the eight steps listed in this chapter and you will be well on your way;

- Start by analysing exactly what pensions and other assets you have that are in place for your retirement;

- Set the income you want to achieve. Be honest about your expectations in retirement. Is this income for survival? Or income for luxury living? Get past the starting point and then see how close you can get to the ideal situation;

- Decide on the best investment structure – inside a pension wrapper or held personally outside a pension;

- Make your asset selection. This must take account of your available capital, risk profile, time to retirement and performance requirements. It's a critical step and one to take with expert advice.

Chapter 12

Take control of your future

We've come to the end of our journey together, you and I. By now, you should have some clarity over the problems within the existing pension system and what you can do to create a better future for yourself.

If I've delivered the right information, then you are ready to start that journey.

Creating an income in retirement that will enable you to do what you have always dreamed of – above and beyond mere 'survival' – and then leave your assets for your heirs, is what many of us would dearly love to do. Before you started this book, you may have been one of many who was nowhere near achieving your vision of a secure future.

Now that you've read what I have to share, I hope that the pathway to a better future has become far clearer and that you are excited about the new track open to you.

Of course, you will need to take responsibility yourself – not give it away to a 'traditional' pension provider. While it will take a little of your time, plus a willingness to make your own investment decisions, the benefits are going to be simply enormous. The journey you are about to start will transform your future.

I'd like to finish by offering you seven key steps to take as you get started.

Start right now

Nothing happens unless you take action. It can be tempting to wait another week or one more year – but, frankly, every day that goes by without action means that you have less time to build the pension you need. This is particularly important if you are closer to retirement age; the growth curve you need to follow leaves no time for delay.

Commission a pension review

If you have an existing pension, commission an independent review right away. It usually takes a couple of weeks to get the key information back from your pension companies and write a report. This information is essential to understanding your current pension's performance, fees and charges, and potential income in retirement.

If you are in a defined benefit scheme, a more detailed report is needed.

If you already know the value of your pension fund and have made the decision to switch to a SIPP, then you can jump the pension review step and go straight to asset selection. You will need to look for the right expert partner to offer a selection of property-related investment opportunities.

Be cautious about advice from IFAs

I'm putting myself right on the line here and taking on the entire financial services establishment. I should apologise to those few forward-thinking IFAs who are willing to step outside the norm and provide the kind of impartial input you have received in this book.

However, most IFAs are trained in the standard pensions model, which is the massive problem I've highlighted throughout this book. What's more, they have to reflect the recommendations of the FSA. As I've already shown, the FSA frowns upon non-regulated investments (including property assets), the concentration of your portfolio in one or two assets, and even the very concept of SIPPs.

So, listen to an IFA with caution and be careful of what 'advice' you take!

Transfer existing pensions into SIPPs (with limited exceptions)

If you already have a pension, then – with certain exceptions – it's time to take control and release the cash value of the fund into a new SIPP that is fit for purpose. You now have the opportunity to improve performance and reduce charges and fees by investing in a much wider range of better performing assets!

Consider investing outside as well as inside the pension system

In most discussions about retirement planning, the extent of the conversation revolves around how much to place within an approved pension scheme. In this book, I have deliberately taken a wider view. For many reasons, it may be appropriate to invest personally – not within a pension scheme. Alternatively, it may be appropriate to have some assets inside the pension system, and other assets outside.

Make the choice based on intelligent decision making and detailed analysis of what you are trying to achieve. Talk to an advisor who understands both possibilities.

Be willing to select assets that offer better growth and income potential

In this book, I have made the case – very strongly, I hope – for placing property and land-related assets in your pension. I 'walk my talk', so to speak, and my own asset base is completely focused on this strategy.

Please take the time to understand why this is my recommendation and what the benefits can be.

Work with experts so you don't have to be one!

If you are like many people planning for retirement, your exposure to the pension system was to commit, many years ago, a monthly sum to your pension plan and then forgot about it. You never took any active part in deciding the investment strategy; in fact, your pension plan never allowed you do that.

In contrast, I'm now expecting you to take responsibility for your future and start making investment decisions that you may not feel competent to make. That's why it will help a lot to work with an expert who can provide input and information mostly about investment options.

Summary

- Take action right now. I know that it's easy to put it off. However, if you want things to change, you have to get going. Don't wait a moment longer!

- Commission a pension review if you have underperforming or frozen pension assets. You need to know what your pension fund is worth and what you could do with it;

- Set up your SIPP if you haven't already done so;

- Take the decision to focus on land and property assets that can deliver the performance you need to achieve your goals;

- Work with experts so you don't need to be one!

About

Axis Property
Investment

My company, Axis, offers a number of services (some of which are paid for, others are provided for free) that are of real and significant benefit to people who are planning for retirement.

Axis is a specialist in sourcing property and land-related investment opportunities within these sectors:

- SIPP-approved property and alternative investments;
- UK residential property;
- USA residential property;
- Student accommodation;
- Hotel rooms, both in the UK and internationally.

What can Axis offer you?

✓ A free, no-obligation pension review, completed by our recommended IFA – but with additional input from Axis.

✓ A free, no-obligation portfolio consultation, designed to assist you with asset selection.

✓ An introduction to an excellent regulated financial advisor who can set up your SIPP for you and arrange the transfer of the cash value from existing pension(s). The advisor will ask for a modest fee for this service, but Axis does not charge.

✓ A detailed strategy consultation conducted face-to-face with a senior investment consultant, covering all aspects of your existing portfolio (or lack of one!) and future plans for retirement. This is chargeable.

✓ A wide variety of excellent value investment opportunities in the sectors noted above. Acquisition fees are payable.

The brief that the Axis acquisition team works to means that everything we offer our clients includes:

Detailed due diligence;

- Fully detailed investment guide and buyers' pack;

- Complete end-to-end assistance with the purchase;

- The very best investment opportunities that combine below-market value pricing, high yields, 'turnkey' operation – including property management, where necessary – and more. We turn down more than nine out of every ten opportunities we investigate, so that only the 'best of the best' are presented to you.

Finally, when making investments of this nature, the need for trust is of paramount importance. In this respect, I should declare that I am a Fellow of the Institute of Chartered Accountants of England and Wales (ICAEW); and Axis is a member of The Property Ombudsman scheme (TPOS), the Office of Fair Trading (OFT) and the International Real Estate Federation (FIABCI).

You can contact Axis by:

Phone: 01273 447 300
Email: pensions@axiscontact.com
Fax: 01273 203 073
Web www.axispropertyinvestment.com

Appendices

APPENDIX 1

Types of pension

There are a variety of pensions in existence. Some are no longer open to new entrants; others are just coming into operation.

Regardless of where the payments come from (usually you or your employer), there are two fundamentally different kinds of pension:

1) Defined Benefit Schemes (also known as final salary schemes)

These are where the pension that you get on retirement is defined by the employer and is fixed. So, for example, you might receive 60 per cent of the average of your last three years' salary, or some other similar calculation.

The idea behind defined benefit schemes is to provide certainty for the employee. Historically, many employees in the public sector and some in the private sector have benefited from these pensions.

The company, or public authority, makes an estimate of what pension pot is required to meet the benefits they expect to pay; it then establishes the contributions – from the employee and the employer – that are needed to create the right size pot.

The main problem is that, as investment returns have fallen, a gap – which is sometimes enormous – has opened up between the size of the pot that is needed to provide the defined benefits, and the actual pot created under difficult investment conditions.

This funding gap, or fund shortfall as it is sometimes described, has caused – and is continuing to cause – huge problems for private and public employers alike.

There are around 6,500 pension schemes (mostly closed to new entrants) that offer defined benefits. According to the Pension Policy Institute, some 3,800 of these schemes (58 per cent) are in deficit. This is extremely worrying!

In the private sector, almost all defined benefit schemes have been closed to new entrants, and a number of companies have gone bust - thus leaving the government to pick up the pieces. More than 100 private schemes are in 'pension protection', which means that the Government will take over the scheme. The problem is that the Government has limited funds and is therefore putting a cap on the maximum pensions that can be paid under the protection program.

As an indication of change, back in 1995 around five million people were enrolled in defined benefit schemes. Today - 2012 - this figure has fallen to one million, of which most are in the public sector.

If you are lucky enough to be within a defined benefit scheme, it is more likely that your existing scheme will be the best pension option there is. However, even within a defined benefit scheme, there are situations where you might want to consider other options, as this book makes clear.

Some defined benefit schemes even include an inflation proof option, which is the 'gold standard' of pensions.

2) Money Purchase Schemes

The majority of pension schemes are so-called 'money purchase' plans. These work on a simple basis:

- You save throughout your working life;

- Whatever the pension pot is on retirement, that's what is available to turn into an income;
- The income will be defined by either annuity rates, if that option is taken, or income drawdown if that option is selected.

Clearly, there is no risk to your employer with this kind of scheme because there is no guaranteed or defined benefit – it all depends on pension performance. This is why, in an era of poor investment performance, most defined benefit schemes have either been closed to new entrants, severely restricted, or placed in pension protection by the Government.

APPENDIX 2

Pension contribution levels and tax relief

For up-to-date information about pension contribution levels and tax relief, please visit: www.pensionsadvisoryservice.co.uk. You should note that details and qualifying amounts change regularly and it is essential that you work with current information. The information in this book is provided as a matter of record only and is not to be construed as personal advice or recommendations of any kind – that can only be provided by a regulated financial advisor.

These notes are a brief summary of key points. They are not comprehensive and are short of precise details that could be critical to your personal circumstances. Therefore, please only consider them a general guide and not to be relied on for decision purposes.

Tax relief

Contributions paid by you into a personal pension plan or a stakeholder pension scheme are made net of basic rate tax (that is, at 20 per cent). This means that for every £100 you want to save, you only pay £80. Tax relief of £20, topping your contribution up to £100, is then added by HM Revenue and Customs (HMRC).

If you are a higher rate tax payer (that is, at 40 per cent), you may able to claim additional tax relief. Depending on how much you earn over the higher rate tax band, any additional tax relief would range from a further one per cent up to a maximum of 20 per cent.

If you are an additional rate tax payer (i.e. at 50 per cent), you may be able to claim additional tax relief at your highest rate from 6 April 2011. Depending on how much you earn over the higher rate tax band and your level of contribution, any additional rate tax relief would range from a further one per cent up to a maximum of 30 per cent.

How are pension investments taxed?

Growth in the value of your pension is free from UK Capital Gains Tax and UK income tax. However, tax on UK dividends cannot be reclaimed.

Annual contribution

The Annual Allowance is an annual limit set by HMRC. Contributions paid in excess of this amount are unlimited but will give rise to a tax charge on the pension scheme member.

In each tax year, a 'relevant UK individual' can pay personal pension contributions that are eligible for tax relief up to the greater of:

- The basic amount (£3,600 for the tax year 2012/2013);
- 100 per cent of your relevant UK earnings for that year.

This is subject to an overall annual limit (the Annual Allowance) – which is £50,000 for the tax year 2012/13. This includes your own contributions and others made on your behalf (for example, from an employer).

Contributions in excess of the Annual Allowance can be made, but will be subject to a tax charge at the your marginal tax rate.

You may be able to pay more and avoid this tax charge if you have any unused Annual Allowance from the previous three tax years. There are carry-forward provisions and I would recommend that you discuss these in detail with your professional advisor.

Lifetime allowance

There is an overall limit on the value of the funds that you can build up in your pension.

Furthermore, there are three junctures at which the value of your fund is checked against this limit – these are called Benefit Crystallisation Events. This events occur at retirement, at age 75 and at death.

In the tax year 2012/2013, the overall limit is £1.5 million.

Any funds in excess of this limit are liable to a tax charge of 55 per cent if taken as a lump sum, or 25 per cent if retained in the fund or made available to provide a taxable income.

Relevant UK individuals

- You are considered a relevant UK individual for pension purposes if:
- You are resident in the UK for tax purposes at some time in the tax year; or,
- You have relevant UK earnings chargeable to income tax; or,
- You were a UK resident for tax purposes sometime in the previous five tax years when you started making pension contributions; or,
- You, or your spouse or civil partner, have general earnings from overseas Crown employment that is subject to UK tax.

Relevant UK earnings

These are normally your total taxable earnings from UK employment and/or self-employment. I would recommend that you contact your professional advisor to clarify things if you have any doubts about what is considered 'relevant' in this respect.

Retirement

- You can take benefits any time after the age of 55;

- You can choose your retirement age at any time up to age 75;

- You may be able to take your investment early if you are medically impaired or you have a protected early retirement age.

What choices do you have on retirement?

- You can normally take a tax-free lump sum of up to 25 per cent of the capital value of your pension pot;

- You can convert your pension into an annuity. However, the income from this is subject to income tax;

- There are many kinds of annuities that can be selected by you;

- Alternatively, you can choose to withdraw an income from your fund directly by arranging income drawdown. I will cover annuities and income drawdown more in Appendix 3.

Death before retirement

If you die before you reach 75 and before taking any benefit from your pension, the total fund can normally be paid as a tax-free lump sum to your estate. This payment is also normally free of inheritance tax.

If you die after the age of 75 but before taking benefits, the total fund can be paid as a lump sum, but will carry a tax charge of 55 per cent.

Alternatively, it can be used to provide a pension for your spouse, civil partner or other dependent.

APPENDIX 3

Options at retirement

As covered in the previous Appendix, you can take normally take retirement at any age from 55 to 75.

The benefits of delaying retirement as long as possible are quite straightforward:

a) Your pension fund can grow considerably larger. Even a few years delay can make a dramatic difference.

b) If you retire at an older age, your life expectancy is shorter. Therefore, the income you can receive from a given pension fund is higher.

The combination of both these factors can make a dramatic difference. Delaying your retirement by even five years may increase your income by 60 per cent or more.

However, at whatever age you decide to formally take retirement, there are two primary options for your UK pension fund: buy an annuity or go into income drawdown.

You should note that these options are the same regardless of the type of pension you have had. So, it makes no difference whether you had a 'traditional' pension scheme or a SIPP.

Both approaches allow you to normally take up to 25 per cent of the fund value – tax free – when you retire.

Lifetime annuities

This is a guaranteed income for (at least) the rest of your life. The key disadvantage of an annuity is that, once you have purchased it, the original pension fund can no longer be inherited by your heirs when you die (with limited exceptions, which I shall look at below).

The second major disadvantage is that any capital growth is reflected in the profit of the company providing the annuity – not in your pocket. While the company will factor in their assumed investment growth when working out how much income to give you, their investment performance may well be below your investment performance if you control the assets!

The annuity can be a **conventional** one, in which the income is either fixed, inflation-linked, or set to increase at a certain rate every year. The more potential increases in the future, the lower the rate of starting income.

Alternatively, the annuity can be **investment-linked**, in which your income rises or falls according to the underlying performance of the fund. Given the hugely disappointing history of pension fund performance over the last 15 years, I would strongly recommend you steer well clear of investment-linked annuities.

As well as these two options, you can choose an annuity that will continue to pay income to your surviving spouse until they die, albeit usually at a rate of 50 per cent of the income that you received. Once again, this kind of annuity will mean that your starting income is considerably lower.

In my opinion, taking an annuity is about the worst choice that most pension savers can make, although it is by far the most common route taken in the UK at the present time.

Value-protected annuities

These will pay out a certain pre-agreed amount if you die before a specified age. The amount paid will represent the difference between the value of the fund and the income that has been received so far. The balance, paid to your estate, will be taxed at 55 per cent.

Here's a simple illustration:

Suppose your pension fund was £100,000 and you took an annuity paying £5,500 a year. If you live for five years after retirement, the fund has paid out £27,500, leaving a balance of £72,500. After your death, this amount would be paid to your estate, with the Government taking tax of 55 per cent. So, that would leave £32,625 to be enjoyed by your inheritors.

Not surprisingly, you will be offered a lower income if you purchase a value-protected annuity because the investment company stands to pay back a considerable sum if you die early. This is factored into their income equation.

Income drawdown

With income drawdown, you can still take your tax-free cash, but you still leave an investment in the pension fund and draw an income directly from this fund.

For the assets I recommend, this immediately places you in a theoretically better position, with the possibility that both the capital value and annual income can continue to grow and may even outpace inflation!

Because your fund is still invested and can suffer from the vagaries of the market, it is possible for your income to go up and down. For this reason, most advisors have only recommended income drawdown for larger pension funds – such as £100,000 and above. However, if you read Chapter Eight on Portfolio Management and consider my views about making the right asset choices, you can see that income drawdown is beneficial with almost all pension funds – provided they are invested in the right choice of assets.

If you are in 'standard' income drawdown, the Government restricts the income you can take to broadly the same as the income from an annuity. Furthermore, if you want to continue making contributions and adding assets to your pension fund, there may be additional restrictions.

With a standard income drawdown, you may not receive a greater income than with an annuity. On the other hand, it still enables your assets to continue to grow through retirement, and also to pass them on to your beneficiaries (with tax consequences).

This is a complex subject and surrounded by many rules. Once again, I strongly recommend that you take professional advice.

Flexible drawdown

If you qualify for flexible drawdown, then you have ultimate control over the taxable income that you take, unrestricted by government limits. In theory, you could sell all your remaining pension fund assets in the open market and draw the entire fund as 'income' in one tax year.

To qualify for this option, the Government has decreed (at least for now) that you must be in receipt of guaranteed pension income of at least £20,000 per year. This income can be made up from any combination of:

- State pension;

- Pension annuities;

- Defined benefit pension income;
- A dependant's pension or annuity;
- Certain types of pensions paid from overseas pension schemes;
- Certain state pensions from other countries;
- Certain payments from the Financial Assistance scheme.

However, it cannot include any non-pension income (i.e. investment or earned)! Also, the £20,000 annual requirement does **NOT** include any income received under an income drawdown plan. To repeat: receiving income under income drawdown does not count towards the £20,000 requirement for flexible drawdown!

Once you are in flexible drawdown, you are prevented from making further contributions to your fund, or building up any further benefits in a final salary pension scheme. You should also note that the £20,000 income requirement may be increased in the future to take account of inflation and other considerations by the Government.

Be careful: your pension provider may not offer flexible drawdown. Of course, if you are running your own SIPP, this restriction does not apply!

Phased retirement

You have the option to convert your pension fund into an annuity or drawdown over a period of time. You can also choose to convert part to an annuity and part to drawdown.

If you have the right sized pension fund, you can consider the option of taking an annuity to make up your pension income to £20,000 per annum – and then convert the rest to flexible drawdown. You may prefer to have your entire fund in flexible drawdown. However, government rules mean that, if you have less than £20,000 guaranteed pension income, then flexible drawdown is not an option. In that case, you may have to choose between an annuity and income drawdown. It's not a difficult choice – in my view income drawdown wins every time.

APPENDIX 4

PASSING YOUR RETIREMENT FUND TO YOUR HEIRS

In this Appendix, I will deal specifically with the issues of what happens to your retirement fund when you die.

The first question is whether you hold the fund within a UK pension scheme, or outside a pension scheme as a personal asset.

Let's start with assets held personally:

Passing on assets held personally to your heirs

You are in full control over any assets you have invested that are outside the UK pension net. You can choose what income you take, when to sell the asset(s), how to dispose of them, and who should inherit part or all of your estate.

If you have substantial wealth, then it is always good practice to take professional advice about matters relating to the disposal of your assets.

Generally, there will be three taxes that need to be considered:

Income Tax – On the profits from any annual income of assets you own;

Capital Gains Tax – On the disposal of any assets prior to death;

Inheritance Tax – On assets left to your heirs on death.

While these three taxes might initially make you feel that it is beneficial to hold assets inside a pension wrapper, this may well be the wrong conclusion. I devoted Chapter Five to discussing the pros and cons of how best to hold an asset. Most of my clients have assets held inside and outside the pensions net because they are trying to balance many different requirements – both for themselves and for their beneficiaries on death.

The overall point about assets held outside the pensions net is you can leave the entire value of your estate to your heirs on death. Yes, there could be inheritance tax to pay, but this only kicks in after the first £325,000 of taxable assets in the estate (2012 figure). In addition, there are ways to mitigate the tax, particularly if you start disposing of assets well before you die.

Passing on assets held inside a UK pension wrapper

This discussion, and the underlying rules, apply to all pension assets – whether a personal or company pension, or a SIPP.

There are three main categories and the rules vary depending on which you fall within. There is also the added complication of whether you have taken an annuity, or are in income or flexible drawdown.

I'll present the 'rules' as clearly as I can. There were major changes in April 2011 that removed the requirement to secure an income by the age of 75.

One important fact to note is that, when lump sum payments are made to beneficiaries on death, these are usually 'discretionary' and are therefore not considered part of your estate for inheritance tax purposes. There may be other tax charges, however, which I shall spell out below.

Death before retirement

At this stage, your pension fund exists but you are not taking income

– therefore, you have not opted for either an annuity or income drawdown.

Death benefits under a personal pension plan or stakeholder scheme are normally paid as a lump sum. Lump sum death payments usually consist of the return of the pension fund that has accumulated, together with any life assurance.

If the lump sum death benefit is paid within two years of the death, it can generally be paid without any tax charges, unless the lump sum exceeds the lifetime allowance (currently £1.5m). It is important that any death benefit is paid within two years in order to avoid any potential tax charges which could be at the 55 per cent rate.

Death benefits do not have to be taken as lump sums. All or part of the lump sum can be used to provide dependants' pensions.

If you have Protected Rights, the situation is more complex. In this case, I would recommend that you take professional advice.

Death after retirement

What can be paid on death depends on what has happened to the pension fund at retirement.

Annuity already being paid

If you already have an annuity in payment when you die, you may have chosen for it to continue to be paid to your spouse or dependant. These annuities are taxed as income.

You may also have elected for value - or capital – protection. This could return a lump sum on death, with the amount varying dependent on how much you have already received as income.

Usually, the amount returned is the difference between the fund value and the amount already paid in income. The lump sum payment is subject to a special tax charge of 55 per cent. Take note that there is a major difference between dying before and dying after you start to draw your pension. If you have not started drawing income, the fund is returned to your estate – but usually no tax is payable. If you die after drawing your annuity, then even with a value protection policy, you stand to lose 55 per cent in tax.

And, of course, if you take a regular annuity and die early, there is no return of any part of your fund on death, regardless of the tax charge!

Pension drawdown

If you choose to enter income drawdown, the balance of any unused fund can be used to:

a) Buy a dependant's pension;

b) Be paid as a lump sum; or,

c) A combination of both options.

Any lump sum on death is taxed at 55 per cent. However, there is an important distinction to be made between this pension drawdown payment and payment under an annuity. With income drawdown, you continue to own the underlying assets. As the fund has increased in value, both from capital growth and possibly not drawing all the income that has accrued, you are entitled to the **FULL** return of the balance of the fund.

This can make a considerable difference. Let's say that you retire at 65 with a fund worth £100,000. You die at age 74, after nine years in retirement:

	ANNUITY	INCOME DRAWDOWN
Value of fund age 65	£100,000	£100,000
Income paid to you	£5,900 pa	£5,900 pa
Income credited to fund	-	£9,000 pa
Net increase in fund from income	-	£3,100 pa
Value of fund after 9 years	£46,900	£169,000
Retained income	-	£27,900
Total value of fund returned	£46,900	£196,900

This is a radical difference made up of a number of elements:

1 Retaining the value of the fund;

2 Choosing assets that generate capital growth and surplus income;

3 Having the right to full repayment.

Clearly, income drawdown is massively beneficial to your dependents, whether they choose to take a lump sum and pay the tax or continue taking income.

If you have protected rights, the rules are again complex and I would recommend that you take professional advice.

If you die without leaving any dependants, the balance of any unused fund on death can be paid as a lump sum to a charity nominated by you. This is tax free.

If your dependant continues with pension drawdown and dies leaving no further dependants of yours, a lump sum may be paid to a charity chosen by your dependant.

APPENDIX 5

USEFUL WEBSITES

Axis Property Investment

www.axispropertyinvestment.com

Register on the Axis website for advance notice of excellent investment opportunities. Read Rod's blog for insightful views about pensions and property investment.

Daily Telegraph

www.telegraph.co.uk/finance/personalfinance/pensions/

Excellent coverage of pension issues with accessible language and (mostly) thoughtful analysis.

Pension Policy Institute

www.pensionspolicyinstitute.org.uk/

Independent comment and analysis on issues relating to pensions in the UK.

Financial calculators?

http://finance.yahoo.com/calculator/index/

Stuck for trying how to work out the future value of an investment, taking into account contributions and interest rates? Try this enormous array of online calculators. They are all designed for the USA, so just think £ rather than $ and you should be fine.

Pensions Advisory Service

www.pensionsadvisoryservice.org.uk

A not-for-profit organisation that provides a host of detailed information about all aspect of pensions (except, of course, what's in this book!). Mostly very readable and accessible.

HMRC (government website)

www.hmrc.gov.uk/pensioners/index.htm

Every kind of detailed information about the rules and taxation of pensions. Good luck finding your way around!